Does GOD Have Favorites?

My Journey through Life Love and Tragedy

Cora Demetra Shannon-Brown

*Priority*ONE
publications

Detroit, MI, USA

Does GOD Have Favorites?

My Journey through Life Love and Tragedy

Cora Demetra Shannon-Brown

Does God Have Favorites?
My Journey through Life, Love, and Tragedy
Copyright © 2025 Cora Demetra Shannon-Brown

All rights reserved. No part of this publication may be reproduced, stored in a retrieval system, or transmitted in any form or by any means – electronic, mechanical, photocopy, recording, or any other – except for brief quotations in printed reviews, without the prior permission of the publisher.

*Priority*ONE Publications, LLC
P. O. Box 361332 | Grosse Pointe, MI 48236
E-mail: info@priorityonebooks.com
URL: http://www.priorityonebooks.com

ISBN 13:   978-1-933972-86-2
ISBN 10:   1-933972-86-6

Editing, Cover, and Interior design by Christina Dixon

Printed in the United States of America

Dedication

I dedicate this book to a lady who was not always understood or appreciated but always and still is loved.
My Mama Louise Rogers Shannon.

I want to thank God

And everyone and everything that touched me in one way or the other so that I have a story and memories to share.

Special Thanks to…
Albert S. Brown
Elmer and Elaine Shannon
Stacey Shannon-Johnson
LC Jr. and Sharon Fuller
Christina Dixon

Table of Contents

Chapter 1: My Childhood in Memphis 9
Chapter 2: Brothers, Sisters, & Family Ties 13
Chapter 3: School Days in Memphis 19
Chapter 4: School at Hyde Park 25
Chapter 5: The Trials of Adolescence 31
Chapter 6: Church, Secrets, & Mama's Control 35
Chapter 7: California Here I Come 43
Chapter 8: High School in Berkeley 47
Chapter 9: Life After High School 59
Chapter 10: Confrontation & Exile 63
Chapter 11: A New Beginning in Oakland 73
Chapter 12: Love & Loss in San Francisco 81
Chapter 13: One Heartbreak After Another 91
Chapter 14: Facing Deception & Heartbreak 99
Chapter 15: Meeting Albert 109
Chapter 16: Beginning a New Life Together 115
Chapter 17: Crossing Oceans, Carrying New Life 125
Chapter 18: Kevin's Arrival 131
Chapter 19: It's Time to Go Home 141
Chapter 20: A Different Kind of Homecoming 145
Chapter 21: Finding a Home in New York 151
Chapter 22: Cross Country Road Trip 155
Chapter 23: Life in New York 161

Chapter 24: Expanding Community Connections 167
Chapter 25: Assembly Lines & Union Tensions...173
Chapter 26: Expecting Geneá..179
Chapter 27: Working for Digital 185
Chapter 28: Back to California 193
Chapter 29: Bustling Streets & Bamboo Headboards......................................203
Chapter 30: Understanding Our Differences 227
About the Author 241

PART 1:

Roots & Beginnings

Chapter 1: My Childhood in Memphis

So, I should start at the beginning. I was told that I was born in an area of Memphis called Hyde Park. For some reason, that always sounded rich to me. Believe me, it was not. I was told that I weighed 13 pounds, and my poor mother couldn't walk for two weeks. After all, my mother was 43 years old, which today is not considered old, but in 1939, when girls were often married by 16 or 17, that was considered old. I was delivered by a midwife named Mollie, as all of us were. They had a paperboy who was fat, and they said I looked like him because of my size. So, I was called "Fats", the paperboy. My first cognizant memory was on Speed Street in an area called Klondyke. This house sat very high with a porch wrapped around it, and there was no barrier to keep you from falling. Of course, I fell off of it and, by some grace, didn't land on the sharp bricks below. I had a dog, and they put him in a box. I heard the word Mange but didn't understand it. All I knew was that he had patches of hair missing, and when Reverend Forster, the minister of our church, came to visit, he began to pick up the dog. I told him to "put he back in the box" because he had the mange. That was so funny to him. I don't know if it was the dog or the way I said it. I remember all of my brothers and sisters living there on Speed Street. They said we had a stream in the back of the house, and that they were always afraid my oldest sister, who was a sleepwalker, would or might fall into it. I learned before my second birthday that my oldest brother had a daughter who was my niece. We were like sisters. They said she was a happy baby, and I was a crybaby. I would only nurse from my mother, and one day, my mother left me with my niece's mother, and they ended up sending my brother downtown to find my mother. I cried myself sick because I would not let her nurse me. I don't remember when I was weaned, but I never drank milk after that. I was so thin and sickly that my aunt, who thought milk was the fountain of life, would try to bribe me to drink just a little. I would try to go around the corner and vomit it up.

My oldest brother's children, nephew Bubba and niece Liz, lived with us. We were all around the same age. I was a bit jealous of them because they always had each other, and I felt all alone. To get attention, I would taunt them by singing a song, "Bubba and Liz fight Cora." I would keep repeating this until an adult acknowledged me and told Bubba and Liz not to fight Cora. As adults, until Bubba passed, the three of us would sing the song I sang as a child. "Bubba and Liz fight Cora. Bubba and Liz fight Cora."

My next memory was of Tully Street. This house was located around the corner from our church and served as the church's parsonage. All the ministers assigned to Trinity had residences and didn't want to live in the parsonage. It was built with a long hall when you entered, and at the end of the hall was the bathroom. There were rooms on each side of the hall. To the right was the church office. Ms. Dixon and Ms. Rhodes would work, making bulletins and other business reports for the church. They later started a kindergarten in the back of the office. I loved Ms. Rhodes. She was kind of plump. She would let me turn the old mimeograph machine. I thought I was the assistant secretary. I liked Ms. Dixon, but she was more businesslike and didn't seem to have the patience of Ms. Rhodes. Of course, I attended kindergarten because it was right across the hall. I never had to get out in the cold or rainy weather. Of course, I was the center of attention. All of the children of Trinity attended kindergarten. At one of the class reunions of Manassas, the school I would have graduated from if I hadn't come to California, one of the young men told the story that I was the prettiest girl in kindergarten. He asked me to kiss him, and I told him no because he had a snotty nose. The whole class howled, and the funny thing about it is that I remember telling him that after all those years. This young man became one of the leading persons in the Social Security Administration and was very helpful in seeing that our people got what was due them.

I had a friend who lived up the street from me, and I called her Muki. Her brother was my brother's friend, and we called him Buddy. To this day, I don't know their real names.

One time, I went home, and Muki came up to me. I didn't recognize her, and she said, "Cora, how could you forget me? I'm Muki."

My Journey Through Life, Love, and Tragedy

I was so embarrassed. Muki and her brother lived up the street in a place we called the Ark. It was built like an Ark, and I didn't know that, at the time, they were welfare recipients. I tell this because they always got their Christmas toys before us, and I didn't think it was right for them to get their toys before me. They would go to the Ellis Auditorium downtown and come back and show me their toys. I never knew why they got them early, but later found out. I always got a lot of gifts at Christmas. It was the most enjoyable time of my life. It was when my brothers and sisters, if possible, would come home. The lady that my aunt worked for always provided the tree, lights, dolls, etc.

One Christmas, my oldest sister, LaRaine, sent me a pink and white Bambi. That was the year the film came out about Bambi, the Deer. That was also the year my brother told me there was no Santa Claus. He showed me the deer and dared me not to tell. I was to act as though I was very excited about it. I was in total confusion and didn't know if I liked the deer because the magic of Christmas had been taken away from me. I, like most people I talk to, say the same thing. They didn't feel the same way about Christmas after they found out there was no Santa. I still wanted to believe it, and processing it took me some time. I just wanted to live in my fantasy world because it was an escape from my reality.

One day, I began to bleed from my nose. My mother and everybody tried everything to stop it. They took blood from my nose and put it into the ground. They pinched my nose. I began to hallucinate, and then they called Dr. A.O. Johnson; I will never forget him because I saw him more than any other person besides my classmates and church members. He came and packed my nose, and then I began to vomit clots of blood. It finally stopped, but I felt like a dishrag. I had no energy. He gave me my usual vitamin B shot and told my mother to give me lots of fluids.

I was always a sickly child who would throw up and have a fever if you looked at me. Would jump out of my skin from loud or unexpected noises. Because of my illnesses, I didn't start school until I was seven years old. I didn't mind staying in kindergarten because it was right across the hall. They finally figured out I had bad tonsils, and they would have to be taken out. Dr. Johnson said we would have to try to wait a year until I could build up enough blood to have them removed. I never got enough blood to satisfy the doctor, but he was afraid I would have another hemorrhage, so they scheduled an operation at the Ear, Nose, Throat, and

Does God Have Favorites?

Eye Hospital in Memphis. At that time, they used Ether to put me to sleep, and I began to spin and spin until I woke up. They gave me popsicles and other cold things to eat. I was in the hospital for two days, and they let me go home. I'll never forget the looks on the staff's faces when I left because my aunt's employer had let her chauffeur come and get me. They had made a bed out of the back seat. It seemed I was not so sickly after the tonsils were taken out, but I still didn't gain any weight. When you were as thin as I was, it was often seen as a sign of economic poverty and not having enough to eat, which was never our case. If we didn't have clothing, we always had food because of my grandparents' farm and my mother's garden.

    We lived on the left side of the hall. We had a living room, a bedroom, a kitchen, and another room that we used as a bedroom. My oldest sister wasn't living with us, but with other friends in South Memphis. She would come and visit sometimes, and one time, she was in the living room with her friend. His last name was Flakes. I thought he was the most beautiful man I had ever seen. I crawled into his lap and proceeded to block any conversation they were trying to have. My sister called my mother and asked if she could come and get me.

    She said, "Come on, Cora, with Mama."

    "No," I told her, because "my name is not Cora but Polly Ann Flakes." I thought my sister would have strangled me if she could because Flakes was so amused that he really didn't want me to go.

Chapter 2: Brothers, Sisters, & Family Ties

I didn't think of or remember my three brothers, who were not there. I never thought of them. My world consisted of who was there at the time. I later found out my oldest brother, whose daughter was my niece, moved to Detroit, and he never returned to Memphis until my mother passed away. My other two brothers went into the service—one into the Army and one into the Navy. So, Marion, my sister, who is 10 years older than me, my brother Sonny (Floyd), and Nick (Elmer) lived on Tully. I was closest to Marion and Nick, and I can't tell you why Sonny was not on my radar. I think it was because he and Nick fought all the time, and I was always on Nick's side. Marion was my second mother, and I called her *my* Marion. She saved me from many punishments.

Nick took the time to talk with me and let me tag along. He threw newspapers, and one morning, I was tagging along, and he was ahead of me, and there was a car coming around the corner and hit Nick. Fortunately, it was ice on the ground, and when he was hit, it was not a thud but a push to save him from the impact. Nick had gotten up and was throwing papers when he realized I was on the ground sobbing, and the poor man who hit him was trying to console me. Nick came back and assured the man he was ok and told me to come on.

Nick was so exciting to me. He and his friend, Buddy, made a clubhouse between the house and the fence next door. You had to have a password to get into the club. Now, I was not allowed to go into the clubhouse. Now, all you had to do was remove the tarpaulin and go in, but for some reason, I thought if I did, he would know, and the other thing he had intimated was that there was something in there that might eat me. One Christmas, I got a play typewriter. It would type. You had to dial every letter and then hit it, and it would type. Nick wanted to use it for his clubhouse, but I told him he couldn't use my typewriter without me being able to go into the clubhouse. That was how I got into this mysterious house. Believe me, there was nothing in it except a tattered rug, a little desk, and, of course, my typewriter. Nick was always into something, and he wanted to play football. My mother was afraid he would get hurt, so he played street football in front of the house and broke his leg, which assured my mother she was right in not giving him consent to play school football. When he got the heel put on the cast, he was playing with the cast and broke the other leg. Well, needless to say, that was the end of his playing football anywhere. He was always thinking, and I was his little sister who adored him.

Sonny was so talented. He played the trumpet. He played so well that he began to play with the older male teachers who played at night to offset their teaching salary. Jim Crow laws didn't care that a minor was playing in a nightclub because, as black children, we didn't count. This playing with adults really ruined Sonny, and again, I will get into Sonny in a later book. He was colorful and born before his time. I do remember hitting Sonny with an ashtray and barely missing his eye. Of course, I couldn't sit for a while without it hurting.

Marion was my love. She was very docile and obeyed. She was my mother's last hope of one of her children finishing college, working as a teacher, and then buying her a brick house. This was the norm among her community of people. Most of her church and neighbor friends' children had accomplished this. I awoke one morning to my mother crying and sitting in a rocking chair. I was confused because I had never seen my mother cry. She wouldn't tell me what was wrong but told me to get ready for school. I obeyed because I was frightened. After all, I had never seen my mother cry. She had also called my aunt Floyd. My cousin Howard was staying with us at the time, and she told him to go to school as well. He told me later that he pretended to leave, but he wanted to find out what was happening. He and Marion were called twin cousins. They were born on the same day and month.

When I returned home from school, Marion wasn't there. I asked my mother where she was, and she said she was going to stay with Aunt Floyd for a while. I didn't believe her but had to accept what she said. Three days passed, and I asked her to call Marion so I could talk to her. She told me that she wasn't home when she called. This went on for a week or so, and I began to throw one of the fits that they said I would do, and she told me Marion was in New Jersey with LaRaine. I began to fall on the floor and kick and scream, and nothing she said would console me. I told her I hated her because she had sent *my* Marion away. I was heartbroken. I cried and cried, and my cousin would make me angry, trying to make me stop by whispering in my ear, "The more you cry, the less you pee." I don't know why he thought I cared. I would cry and rock myself for hours. I guess you could say this was the beginning or the seed of the title of my book. I had lost the most precious person besides my brother. She would be the one who would pay attention to my cries and soothe me. I wasn't loyal to her. I felt I had let her down. I say this because Marion was having an affair with a man who lived down the street from us. We would have to pass his house to get to church or go to the little corner store for things. My mother did not like this man, and she knew Marion was seeing him on the side. My mother had Marion's future already picked out. She was to finish LeMoyne College, marry the minister of music at our church, find a teaching job, and buy us a house so that we could move up and live happily ever afterward. She would send me with Marion any time we had to pass this man's house, and she would tell me to tell her if she stopped or talked to him. Marion would try to bribe me by buying me my favorite sour pickle, not to tell. I had the best intentions not to tell, but for some reason, my mother could always get me to tell. I really felt bad about tattling on Marion because I truly loved her as a sister, and she was so kind and good. All of that didn't stop her from getting together with this man. She secretly married him, and when she found out she was pregnant, she had to tell Mama. That was the cause of all the crying that morning when I awoke. That was when the decision to send her away was made because they had done everything to keep her from him.

    Nick and I continued to attend school, and when I graduated from the third grade, we moved back to Speed Street. I was happy to leave Tully because, just before we moved, I was almost bitten by a rabid dog. He came down the street frothing at the mouth, and I ran to the first house I could get to, but there wasn't anyone home. I ran to the next house, but they weren't home either. However, I managed to get between the screen and the door just as I heard someone banging on something, and the dog began to run toward the noise. I think they killed the dog. It set up a fear of dogs, and I never really wanted a dog or any other pet. The last thing I remember about Tully was my brother Charles coming home from the war. My other brother stayed in Cincinnati when he got out of the military service. He came home later with his new wife. I was so excited to see him because I didn't remember either of them. He and his wife had bought a Hudson car, and I remember everybody saying it was built like an upside-down tub because when you got in it, you had to step down into it. My mother cooked and bought all kinds of snacks. I got to eat vanilla wafers and cheese, and I ate and ate out of nervousness. No one paid me any attention because they were all preparing. I got so sick and began to vomit, and of course, my mother thought it was just another one of my vomiting spells, so she gave me ginger ale and put me to bed, so I didn't see them until the next day. I didn't get much attention because my brother was busy visiting friends from years ago, and my mother was busy attending church. It became a big thing that my sister-in-law felt ignored and unwelcome, and a rift existed there for as long as I could remember. I finally convinced all of them that I was a child, and I didn't know anything about what happened, didn't care, and didn't blame either of them. We finally became friends. I remember my mother playing matchmaker for my brother Charles with one of Marion's friends who lived up the street from us and was in my mother's young adult Sunday School class. They finally got married, and I was their flower girl.

Part 2:

Growing Up in Segregated Memphis

Chapter 3: School Days in Memphis

I transferred to Klondyke School. Nick stayed at Manassas. That's when I joined a little dance troupe that performed at the Black Cotton Carnival, an annual event called the Cotton Maker's Jubilee.[1] The Jubilee was more than just a parade—it reclaimed space for African Americans in a city whose official festivals excluded them, and their contributions to the cotton industry. It fostered leadership, culture, self-worth, and civic engagement through symbolic royalty and community-wide participation. Today, Carnival Memphis includes this legacy in its broader celebration, symbolizing both a merging of traditions and historical reconciliation.

In my day, the Jubilee started on some streets in South Memphis and ended on Beale Street. All the white folks, especially the men, would stand at the corner where the parade turned onto Beale Street. The bands and majorettes would really perform. The majorettes would call pop the corner, and each girl tried to outdo the other. Well, naturally, this caused their skirts to fly, and the men could get a good look up their legs. Of course, the men would laugh, point, and make inappropriate gestures, but they were white and could do or say anything they wanted. Our dance troupe took second place, but we protested because we received an encore, while the first-place group did not. As always, there are favorites among all the judges. It was the same when Ms. Hightower sponsored me for junior king and queen of the Carnival. We had to raise money; the one who raised the most was the crowned queen, and the princess came in second. Of course, after investing a lot of money, I came in second and was crowned princess. They said the princess was supposed to serve the

---

[1] Memphis Cotton Makers' Jubilee Collection, The University of Alabama Libraries Special Collections http://archives.lib.ua.edu/repositories/3/resources/4906 Accessed August 23, 2025.

Does God Have Favorites?

Queen. I knew that wasn't going to happen. We rode in a coach, and she had to put her own robe in, as I did mine. I never thought of her as queen. I was queen, and that was that.

My next memories were back on Speed Street again. This time, I was older and was friends with a girl who lived three houses across the street from me. Her father worked at the Lowenstein Department Store in the candy division, and he brought home these sugar eggs with an opening and scenes in them. They were the most beautiful things I had ever seen. Her mother was very fair with beautiful hair, and her father was very dark and had a cock eye, as we used to call them. My mother never liked the idea of my spending the night away from home. As I mentioned earlier, she was controlling in my upbringing. So, we would stay out until dark and then walk each other back and forth until one of our mothers called us in for the last time. We then would walk to the middle between our houses and say our goodbyes.

Some Mexican people lived directly across from us. We knew the man was Mexican, but we didn't know what ethnic group the woman was from. She had a disease, I guess, that caused her skin to peel on her face and leave it pink underneath. According to my family, she made the most wonderful tamales, and it was said in jest that you didn't know if one of those scabs might be in them. It seemed the taste of her food was so good that it overrode the fear.

Then, it was our neighbor to the left of us who had my mother teaching us never to take candy or anything else from strangers. It seems this woman told my mother that one of her two boys would swell up every full moon until sometimes his skin would burst. Someone told her to take him to a woman in Mississippi because someone had put a hex on him. I thought of Richard Pryor telling his story about Ms. Rudolf when I heard this. She told my mother that this woman told our neighbor who had done this to her child and why, and gave her this medicine to give to him that looked like tar. She gave it to him, and he never swelled up again. So, this made me afraid to take candy from any stranger. Down the street from that neighbor was a dark, dank, and very scary house. A blind woman lived there, selling sodas, chips, candy, and other little knick-knacks. I never knew how she could tell what you were buying or give you change, but I never stayed there any longer than I had to, and I always took someone with me.

My Journey Through Life, Love, and Tragedy

It wasn't long before Mama was in a tizzy because we had to move again. The people who owned that house on Speed died, and the children wanted to sell it. Of course, we didn't have the money to buy it, so it was a worry every day until my aunt and mother found a house on Randle three streets over. This was still in the Klondyke neighborhood, so it didn't upset my school. My brother Sonny had joined the Marines. My brother Charles, his wife, Nick, and I were the ones who lived on Randle. The one exciting thing that happened on Randle Street was that my sister-in-law and brother had a beautiful baby boy. He was gorgeous. He had very large, beautiful green eyes. My mother babysat him along with my brother and me after we got out of school. My mother would be sick, and she would have my brother put the bed against the wall and supply the diapers and milk so she could sit with him. We all doted on this child. My brother, Nick, almost cut off his finger in shop class at school while trying to make a potty chair for the child. I was a wreck when they told me Nick was at the hospital, and I cried until he came home. They were able to save his finger, but he was never able to stretch it out completely again because it had cut into a tendon.

One day, while I was in school, I was told to go to the principal's office. When I got there, there were four of my classmates there. Two plainclothes police officers questioned us about walking in this woman's yard. There was an old lady who sat at her window every day, and if you stepped on her lawn, she would take her cane, tap the window, and shake it at you. The only reason we would step on her lawn was that there was mud instead of a sidewalk in front of her house, and if we stepped into the street, the safety council would report us. We felt doomed. So, the officers questioned us, and we were all crying, saying we didn't walk on her lawn, except one girl named Sally Coe. She was tough, and she wouldn't cry or give in. So, they said they would take us to the old lady's house so she could identify us. Of course, at the time, we didn't know that this was a scare tactic because they were tired of this woman calling down to the station. She really had nothing else to do. They put all five of us in the back seat of their car. We cried so much that we fogged up the windows. They had her look out of the window to identify us. Sally never cried, and she stood her ground, saying that she did not step on her lawn. They brought us all back with red eyes and trembling. I was too afraid to tell my mother for fear of getting a whipping. She would have considered this an embarrassment. When talking about this later as an adult, everybody is appalled at how the officers were allowed to come on campus, put us in a car, and take us off campus without permission from our parents. The principal was aware of this and allowed it. This goes to show you how much times have changed. They also called us out of class and inoculated us without permission. I'm happy and grateful to know today that they didn't give us smallpox or syphilis or any other experiments that were done on Black Americans.

I didn't have a relationship with God as I do now, but I joined the church and was baptized. This was an accepted practice, and if I hadn't, my mother would have been very upset. As I remember, this was the only time I remember her smiling with pride when I stepped up and said I accepted Christ. I was nine years old and didn't know what that entailed, but I knew it would make her happy.

My sister-in-law graduated from LeMoyne, Memphis's Historically Black College, with a BA degree and immediately started teaching. She got an assignment at the same school as my aunt. She taught first grade and had my father make her a sandbox. She was the only teacher to have one. She was a very good teacher. Today, one of my very dear friends said she would never forget her because she was in her class, and the class went to the zoo. She soiled her pants, and my sister-in-law took her to the restroom, cleaned her up, and put clean underwear on her. She said no one ever knew she soiled her pants. She was eternally grateful for that and to her. They moved to South Memphis to a newly developed neighborhood for "coloreds," and then she got pregnant with her daughter. She was a living doll. They dressed her in the finest clothes, and she always looked like a living doll. They now had two children. They began to move on up.

We had to move again, and this time, it was to an area my mother thought was beneath her. It was considered part of the city, but it looked rural like the country, and she considered the people to be from the country, and not in her league. It was in an area called Hollywood. It was far away from everything we belonged to, and we didn't have a car, which made it all the more unattractive to her. The house belonged to my uncle, who was married to my mother's sister. His family once owned that whole city block where this house and lot were located. He sold all of the properties except this piece. It was probably because it was the lot that his family's home was on. My parents had no other place to go, so we moved to Hollywood on Dexter Street. As far as my mother was concerned, she felt the way I felt sometimes that God had abandoned her. All her children were married and lived in different cities or other parts of town, leaving Nick and me.

    My mother was very smart and knew things that were amazing when I think about what she did. The house didn't have sheetrock; the walls were just bare wood. She sent my father to the hardware store, and she bought a material called felt. It was put over the plank and acted as sheetrock. She then wallpapered over the felt. The house had an indoor toilet but no tub or running hot water. My father had to try to connect the gas stove so she could cook. Unfortunately, we were too late to get the part he needed, so she took a bucket, put charcoal in it, put a grate on it, and we had hamburgers that first night. From then on, she could cook. We had a wringer washing machine on the back porch, but we never had the money to install a water heater. Instead, we relied on a very large tea kettle. They also bought a tin tub, which was the size of a regular tub. When we bathed, we heated the tea kettle, poured in hot water, and then added cold water until the water temperature was just right for a bath. We did that until I left home for California. We had a heater in the living room. The house had a living room, a dining room that doubled as a bedroom, a kitchen, a toilet, and a bedroom. The bed I got when we lived on Tully was at the foot of my parents' bed, and Nick slept in the dining room. My mother raised chickens. My brother had to raise them until they became older because my mother couldn't stand to touch them as chicks. She had a garden on the lot next to the house, and she and our neighbor, Ms. Blackwell, would exchange vegetables for whatever the other didn't raise. There were no sidewalks, and a ditch ran in front of the house. My mother went and got a slab of concrete to cover the ditch and stepping stones to the house, so we didn't get mud on the porch. The porch went across the front of the house. We had two gliders, one on one end of the porch and one on the other. It was customary to sit on the front porch, although my mother seldom did. She would come out only when she didn't want people in the house. My father sat on the porch all the time.

    When it came to chores, I hated washing clothes because, inevitably, no matter how careful I was, I would get my hand caught in the ringer. I also hated hanging clothes because my mother used to have everything hung together: all the sheets, pants, shirts, and so forth.

Chapter 4: School at Hyde Park

    I was enrolled at Hyde Park School in the seventh grade. My mother always took me to school and introduced me to the class and the teacher. I would be so embarrassed. She would say, "I present to you Cora Shannon, a new student at your school."

    Well, this school was not of the same social class she was used to, and they all snickered and laughed. The teacher told them to be quiet and thanked my mother. She would walk home, and the school was quite a long walk. We had to pass a white school to get to our school. I never cared about going to a white school or even associating with them. We had our own community, and there was always something to do. I was in my own little world and really didn't realize the depth of segregation. I liked my school, except when I first got there. It seemed every girl had burned or pressed their hair to nubs. I seemed to be the only one with long hair, and they would unbraid it and dare me to braid it back. This was very new to me because I had never gone to school and had an altercation that would lead to a fight because my mother didn't allow us to fight. She thought it was barbaric. She would go to the mother of the kids and talk to them, and this didn't happen again until another bully challenged me. When I transferred to Hyde Park there was another student named Ernestine Willett. Her boyfriend was Edgar Smith. When I came to the school, Edgar asked me to be his girlfriend, and we started going together. I didn't know he was her boyfriend. She said she heard I wanted to fight her. That was the bait. My friend Rachel told me that if I let her beat me up, she would beat me up, and Rachel was big. I was petrified. I couldn't tell my mother this time because I would lose my status in the school as a snitch and mama's girl. So, it came to the day we were supposed to fight, and if you can imagine, we were in a Girl Scout meeting, and she was looking at me, telling me she was "going to beat my ass." So, after the meeting, of course, we all went out the back door because the janitor had locked the front door. We were surrounded in a circle when we got outside, and someone pushed her into me. I had a baton that had lead in it, and I hit her on the head with it. She ran off crying, and I was crying too because I thought I had damaged her head. Her mother would come to school, and I would be in trouble both at school and at home. It was over. The next day, she came to school with a small bandage on her face, but no more fighting. It was years later, at the reunion that I mentioned earlier, that she came up to me and said, "I heard you wanted to fight." We both laughed and hugged each other.

    One year, we had a talent show, and I sang *I Saw Mommy Kissing Santa Claus* and brought down the house. I had a new respect. Mr. Omar Robinson asked me to be in the Glee Club. I soon became a soloist, and we sang at different functions around the city. We sang one song that was very high and took a lot of voice to sing. We were invited to this church in an area further out than Hollywood called Douglas. We were to sing for some dignitary. I can't remember who he was, but I think he was the first colored someone in government, and it seemed to me that people always fawned over people because of their positions, wealth, and name. I always rejected that. That is something that upsets me to this day. I admire people's accomplishments, but that's it. They are still just like the rest of us humans, trying to make it on this little ball of mud called Earth. They are no more or less. This person was so late that they had us sing our songs, and we were about to collect our things when he showed up and asked that we sing again for him. I immediately said no to Mr. Robinson, and my mother gave me the evil eye; I then capitulated. But I didn't put my heart into it as I did the first time we sang it. I thought he had disrespected us by being late and not offering an apology, and then demanding we sing again.

    I have to acknowledge Mr. Robinson. He was gay, but I loved him because he was so talented. He played for churches and other functions. He built a house for himself and his mother. Sadly, he ended up in a field, killed and dismembered. His dental records were the only means of identification. It was written in Jet magazine. I truly cried because he didn't deserve that. One of the young men they arrested said he begged for his life. Again, I cried and asked why. Everybody knew he was gay, but no one cared or mentioned it. I never gave it a thought. I just loved hearing him play.

One day, we were coming off the playground, and I decided to go the front way. In this car was a white male with his private parts exposed. I ran inside, but he was gone by the time I got inside. I wondered, with him being white, what they would have done, being that I was just a colored girl?

Junior High Graduation

It was time for graduation, and all the girls were instructed to wear white dresses. I had seen this dress I wanted, and Ms. Blackwell next door would make it. My mother went and got this flimsy nylon material, and it was too flimsy to make the dress I wanted. I really didn't want to march, but Ms. Blackwell did such a good job on the dress. She made me feel better, but I was still disappointed. I look back now, and I am ashamed because my mom did the best she could. I'm sure the material I wanted was way out of budget. I really didn't know the depths of our poverty until I got older. After graduation, our class went to the Memphis Zoo. Thursdays were the colored day to go to the zoo. I didn't enjoy myself because they said the boys had a snake that they were throwing at the girls, so I stayed near the front with the teachers. I am definitely afraid of snakes, rats, and mice. I have phobias of them.

My mother would clean the house from top to bottom twice a year in the winter and spring. We had to take the rugs out and beat them, polish the furniture, scrub the floors, and work all day. One day, we started cleaning, and my mother's nose began to bleed. She would sit for a while, and it would stop. Every time she got up to do anything, it would start to bleed. It began to gush, and she was going through towels like they were tissue paper. We called our aunt, and she came, and we finally had to call an ambulance to take her to the hospital. She had a cerebral hemorrhage. They brought her home, but she was in a coma. We had to turn her every fifteen minutes to keep her blood from clotting in her brain. My sister-in-law sat by her bedside all night. Everybody took turns but me. She awoke, looked around, and said that her linen was dirty, and directed me to go and iron her a clean sheet. I was taught to "iron on all six sides" by folding the sheet a certain way. I thought I had ironed it the way she taught me. When I finished, I took it to her, and she threw it in my face and told me to iron the sheet. I guess it passed the second time because she allowed them to change her linen.

My mother believed that cleanliness was next to Godliness, and she was a stickler about dirt. I think of my mother today and her life, and how much she missed. My mother loved soft ice cream, but she never bought it because she had to go to the side window. She never went to a movie because she could not climb the stairs. The colored section was in the area right under the projector. I often say they should have gone to the movie instead of making me. It is always in jest.

Part 3

Coming of Age

Chapter 5: The Trials of Adolescence

One summer, Harry came home from Detroit, which began our relationship. He gave me a boxing glove necklace with an emerald-cut diamond in it. Stupid me gave it back because of Rufus. He told me he was talking to another classmate of mine. I didn't realize his intention until I gave it back, and he began to make his move on me. It was too late because Harry left and went back to Detroit. I never saw that necklace again, and when I asked him about it, he didn't remember.

It was time for me to go to high school, and my mother refused to let me go to Douglas, not only because she thought it was inferior, but also because it was a tradition that all the Rogers and Shannon families had attended and graduated from Manassas. So, we used my aunt's address in Klondyke. I found out later that a lot of us went to Manassas instead of Douglas. That gave me comfort because we had to catch three buses to get to Manassas. One day, as we had boarded the last bus, it was filled to the front. A white man got on, and the bus driver told us Negras to move back. One of the boys said, "There was nowhere to move." The bus driver got off the bus, went to the pay telephone, and called the police. They got on with their billy clubs and began pushing us until we were packed like sardines. They told us we had better not move until we got to our stop. Some of the girls began to cry because one of their ankles was smashed, and she had to be carried off the bus. I was terrified of the police because I saw what they could do, and we were helpless.

Manassas went from first grade to twelfth grade. It was divided by French doors. The elementary school was on one end, and the high school was on the other. We had an auditorium, a shop, a home economics room, and a band room. We did not have a gymnasium. We had an open field where the guys played and practiced football.

I always wanted to be a majorette and an opera singer. I would practice both. I taught myself to twirl a baton, and I would march in the open lot for hours. Then, I would make up songs and pretend I was at the Met singing in Italian and any other language I made up.

Manassas had a choir, band, and football. I don't remember basketball, but I'm sure they had it because my aunt played basketball when she went to Manassas.

In the home economics department, we spent one semester learning sewing and the other half the school year learning to cook. Every Friday, we cooked beans and cornbread for the football team. The boys had wood shop. I was told after taking the strings loose from an apron until the holes began to show that I should stick to cooking. I don't think I have the patience to sew because later in life, I tried to sew and cut out the pattern of a skirt with two backs.

The most important thing Manassas had was a sense of pride and community, and they always celebrated Black History. Manassas didn't have the amenities that I found in Berkeley, but it had teachers who cared that you get the best of what they had to give. I learned later that, academically, Manassas was superior to Berkeley. Because they didn't have a swimming pool, green room, or gymnasium they concentrated on educating you in things that would allow you to work teaching or helping others. They all knew that education was the secret to our future, not as individuals but as people. The teachers all knew who you were by your last name. Most of them grew up with my family, so the expectations of being a Shannon was very important at Manassas.

Impacted by Colorism
The drum major for the band went to our church, and she told me what day they were having tryouts. I was so nervous and excited. A friend asked me where I was going, and I told her. Like a nut that I am, I suggested she try out, too. Although she was stiff as a board and I outmarched her, she got on the team, and I didn't. She was lighter than I was, and her hair was a little longer. That example seems to have followed me all my life. I never thought I wouldn't get it because I was a better marcher. I didn't know the color division was so evident among my people. I can't begin to tell you my world crumbled. I was so disappointed that I asked my aunt if she would appeal to this teacher, and of course, my aunt said no because they didn't get along.

My Journey Through Life, Love, and Tragedy

Another friend saved me from complete despair. She said, "You don't want to be cold out there with those skimpy outfits," but I did.

"Come on and join the band," she encouraged.

"I only play piano," I told her.

She said, "You can play the bells."

She took me to Mr. Horne, who knew my brother and family, and told us that he had someone on the bells and gave me a flute.

He said, "Pretend you are blowing into a bottle." Then he showed me the fingering. "Take it home, and next week, I want you to play this song on the flute."

I returned the next week and barely played the song. But he told me to go and pick out my uniform. I could tell he wanted more than my playing the flute. I was flattered, although he was way too old for me, but my ego was being boosted. And since I could only go to school and church, I guess girls find encouragement and choose to be around whoever is available to them.

I remember the band and choir were invited to perform at Lane College in Jackson, Tennessee. I felt really special because I could ride on either bus, and of course, I chose the band bus. They were more boisterous than the choir members. It was 1955, during the time they had killed Emmett Till. The boys on the bus made up a song about it. I think they were trying to be funny because they were petrified but didn't want to show it.

My friend Delores was scheduled to play *The Flight of the Bumble Bee* on her clarinet. I asked her if she had practiced, and she said, "Naw." She played the song so well that she got a standing ovation. She and her whole family were very talented. Her brother became a famous jazz artist.

I noticed on the bus that my friend who made the majorette team was not there, nor had she been at the last two games. I found out she had only marched twice. Her mother said it was too cold for her to be in those skimpy costumes. I didn't know whether to laugh or gloat. I did neither because I was happy where I was, and I got a standing ovation in the choir. Getting into the band and choir was the same scenario at church as far as the attention I would receive from the pastor. One other important thing about Manassas and the community is that we had two churches that provided our school with all-new uniforms for football and band. We always had hand-me-downs from the white schools, but we would practice in them. When we marched or played football, we had brand-new uniforms. Both churches would have dinners and programs to raise money for the school. I had to mention that because I find it so important that they wanted us to have the best.

Messed Up for Life

I started my period when I was 13, and I was happy because the ignorance of knowing my anatomy led to all sorts of crazy ideas. It was believed that if you didn't start by 18, the blood would blow your brains out, and since my cousin started at nine and all my brother's girlfriends had their periods, I just knew I might suffer the fate of the blood blowing out my brains. I started my menses on Good Friday, and when I told my mother I was bleeding, she ran through the house shouting, "Oh, you messed up for life!" I thought I defied the brain thing by starting, but now I was messed up for life. I was 18 years old before I understood what she was talking about. I could now have babies. She sent me to the store to buy pads and a belt. I didn't know what to buy; they had many different kinds. Thankfully, Mr. Culver, the store's owner, showed me what to buy. I came home, and Mama showed me how to put them on; she also said I was to burn them when I took them off because people could get them and run me crazy using voodoo. I had to take newspapers to wrap my pads in and bring them home. The next day, I had a hair appointment. The beauty shop was in the parsonage where we used to live. I couldn't get my hair washed because if you washed your hair, bathed, or got wet, you may catch a cold or, worse, go out of your mind. The beautician would put this stuff that smelled like gasoline on your hair to clean it. I took the bus to the beauty shop and stayed there all day. I didn't know that I should have brought pads. My pad was soaked, and when I went to the restroom, there were clots, and I thought my insides were coming out. I asked the beautician if she had a pad, and she said she didn't. She was a woman and had three girls, and she couldn't or wouldn't give me a pad. I put tons of toilet tissue over the soaked pad. When my brothers came to pick me up, and I was walking like a handicapped person, my brother Charles asked Nick what was wrong with me because he wanted me to hurry up. Nick told him I had started my period, and he didn't say anything else. I got home, and Mama put me to bed. The next day, I had a crook in my neck because I slept with my head hanging off the bed. It was Easter, and I had always wanted to save my curls.

Chapter 6: Church, Secrets, & Mama's Control

    We got a new pastor who began to flirt with me. I played the piano for Sunday School, and there were steps next to the piano that led to another set of steps, which in turn led to the sanctuary's level. He would come by where I was playing the piano and ask if I was going to say hello to my pastor, and I would half respond. I knew he was flirting with me, and I played coy. He then called me into his office and asked me to take the Sunday School census. He also began to take Pearlie and me to sing at events he spoke at and funerals he officiated. My aunt was suspicious and would always complain about her class being interrupted to take the census. It was well known in Trinity and other churches that most ministers always had a woman on the side. At our church, it was a lady who served as secretary for at least three to four ministers. He ignored her in that position and concentrated on me. He had the phone company put a switch on his phone so that when he was talking to me, none of the extensions could be heard. He flattered me, and I felt good about myself. No one else ever said I was pretty. My mother would say I had a crooked head, and she would get really angry when trying to make a straight part when she combed my hair. She also said I had a bell pepper nose. Although I always thought I was the bomb, those comments really stuck. I would always pinch my nose to try to make it smaller. We decided to have a code name, and I called him Ed. So, no one would know who I was talking about. From that point on, I wanted to go to church.

    The lady who was always the minister's woman wrote a letter to my mother telling her she should be aware that the minister was molesting me. My mother didn't believe it at first, but I think after I left for California, she began to listen to the whispers. Mama adored this pastor, and they talked every day. She was head of the No. 1 Stewardess Board, and one of their functions was to take care of the pastor, his family, and the parsonage. She had a relationship with every church pastor, but for some reason, this one had her mesmerized.

As I said, my mother was really controlling. All my friends and nieces could go to the movie after church. I had to choose between staying at church for a program or going home. I later found out there were two reasons for this. One, my mama had no money to give me for the movie, and secondly, she was afraid of my catching the bus alone. Where we lived in Hollywood was unusual in terms of its location on a map. Hollywood Street ran north and south, and it ended at one end at Chelsea. On the other end, it ran out at Jackson. From Chelsea to the first set of railroad tracks lived white people. From that set of tracks to another set of tracks lived colored people. From the last set of tracks to Jackson lived white people. Most of the time, the bus from Chelsea to Dexter Street ran every now and then, and most of the time, we just walked to Chelsea, which meant we walked through the white neighborhood. It was on the fringes, but it was still white. Because of this, I never got to go anywhere that would put me in that position at night. Another reason for her fears was being made to watch her neighbor's son being lynched and burned. She would sometimes wrinkle up her nose and say that it smelled like flesh burning. She was made to watch this at the age of 11. She also witnessed the Klan attack my grandfather when he walked to church with his bible, and they dislocated his shoulder. My mother had my brother buy a TV to encourage me to want to stay home. I enjoyed watching TV, especially the Mouseketeers, but I wanted more.

Church and school remained my world. I forgot that going to the country to see my grandparents every Saturday was the other part of my world. We went every Saturday to take my grandparents' staples because they no longer had cows for milk and butter. We would stop at a store named Robilios. The name always fascinated me. We would get what they asked for and get my grandfather fishhook tobacco. I remember it clearly because the package had a red hook on it. My grandparents were the most loving and beautiful people in my life. We called them "Mama and Papa in the country," and we would say the whole name every time we referred to or called them. I guess since we also called our parents Mama and Papa, we added *in the country* to distinguish them from one another. Everybody in the family called them that. Papa in the country was a very God-fearing man who raised his family and was very clannish. It was his wife and children who made up his world. I loved him because of his gentle spirit. He was coming in from the pasture one day when the old mule, Sadie, kicked him on the ankle. Papa in the country had diabetes, and I wanted to kill Sadie for kicking my grandfather. He adored his girls. My mother, being the oldest, was named after his mother, Louise. He had ten brothers and one sister. Mama in the country was feisty and could cook so well that I even ate her food. I remember her letting me churn the butter, but I would only be allowed a little time because I wasn't strong enough to beat the milk into butter.

  She had a wooden mold with a palm tree on top, and she would put the butter into the mold, which was so yellow and pretty. She could sew very fine stitches, and the quilt I have now is one of the last quilts she made. I loved her because she would make me feel special, and she would tell me I was special. I never liked my name, Cora, but I loved her so much that I came to like it. My grandparents were sharecroppers, and when I was a little girl, I overheard my grandfather tell my aunt that he hadn't made any money that year from the crop. My aunt and her sisters and brothers came together, purchased nine acres of land, and built a house for their parents. My aunt Katie was the only one of them who was a professional. The rest of them were waitresses, butlers, maids, and cooks. That was so amazing to me. The only thing was that when they bought the land, they had no easement to it. They convinced the white family that lived on the main road to allow them to use a section of their property to cut a lane to their parents' property. The penal farm and old folks' home were on the other side of the lane. There were many Saturdays when they had to hook their team of horses to pull the car out of the lane. They were never able to put rocks or some material that would keep us from getting stuck in the mud. I would get very frightened when we got stuck. That was why I didn't want to go when it was raining or had rained. There was no getting out of going to the country because my mother didn't want me to be home alone. The older I got, the more I balked about going. I wanted to stay home and watch TV or just be by myself. I loved my grandparents, but I was bored as I got older. I wasn't allowed to be in the conversation and didn't know what or who they were discussing, so I sat on the porch until it was time to go.

  There was one Saturday my mother relented and let me stay home. Well, wouldn't you know that two of the boys in the neighborhood came by and saw me sitting on the porch? They came and asked if I would give them some water. Just as I was bringing them the water, I saw my aunt's car coming down the street. I knew my mother would have had a hissy fit seeing them on the porch. They were not inside, but the porch was too close for her. I told them they had to run out of the backyard and jump the fence because my mother would suspect they had been in the house, and we had done something bad. They obeyed because they didn't want their parents to know either.

I remember when my brother was attending Tennessee State, and they had homecoming every year in Memphis. My cousin was visiting from Chicago, and he planned to take us both, as well as his girlfriend, to the homecoming. I didn't have anything to wear because the last dress I got, which I called a mourning dress. It was grey, trimmed in black up to the neck and below the knees, with long sleeves. It was perfect for a funeral. My cousin had a powder blue sheath with gold buttons up the sleeve and down the back, and a stole on one shoulder. My brother's girlfriend said she would bring me one of her dresses to wear. It was a cute little black sheath with spaghetti straps and a bolero lace that covered the bust line. Mama waited until I got dressed, and we were getting ready to go when she asked, "Where are you going?"

"With Nick to the homecoming dance," I answered.

Well, she didn't want me to go, and she knew how to play me. I didn't get it until I was much older that she always got what she wanted, which at that moment was for me not to go.

"You are not going out of here looking like a Jezebel; if you don't wear your dress, you are not going."

Jean, Nick, and his date tried to tell me to put it on, and I could change it later. I was not having it, and I played right into her hands. She never wanted me to go to the homecoming dance. She never wanted me to go anywhere. I would ask to go and promise to do what she said, and she would say I know you will. I would ask, "How do you know that?"

"Because you are not going," she would say.

I would get so angry with her. She had my brother buy a TV, thinking that would abate my desire to go places. My family always thought I wasn't worldly and was unaware of a lot of things in life. Little did they know.

One day, my mom said that my sister Marion was going to a conference in Los Angeles, and she was bringing the two oldest of her children with her to stay with us until she returned. My mother said if I helped her with them, she would let me go back to California with my aunt and uncle when they came to Memphis. I thought to myself, *this is it. This is my chance, I will never come back.*

After visiting California once, I knew I would live there someday, once I had the chance. I did everything she asked, even if it meant standing on my head. That's what I would do.

I'll never forget my nephew. He would get so bored that he would say, "Grandmother, there's nothing to do."

My aunt would tell him, "Go wipe off the car."

"That's nothing to do!" he would say.

We laughed and laughed. He was and still is very smart today. When my aunt and uncle came, and I was allowed to go back with them, I packed everything I could, knowing I would not be coming back. They would have to hog-tie me and drag me back.

Part 4

Stepping into Independence

Chapter 7: California Here I Come

I wanted to get away from the pastor and the band leader. I wanted to go to school and be free. I always like the relaxed atmosphere in Berkeley. There were no judgments and standards to live up to. There was no protocol. I wanted to be free. I didn't want to have to go to church in the rain. One Sunday, Mama sent me to church, and when I was waiting on the second bus, the rain came down in sheets. I could hardly see, and if I didn't stand exactly at the bus stop, they would pass me up, sometimes even if the bus driver saw me standing there. We were at their whims and wants. The bus didn't come, and I stepped inside the doorway near the bus stop. I was still getting soaked. I ran over to a lady's house across the street from where I was standing. She was a member of my church, and she lived with her husband over the funeral home they owned. It took a long time before she answered, and I began to panic. She finally opened the door and was appalled when she saw me. I asked her if she was going to church and if I could ride with her. She said she wasn't going to church that day, but she would see if there was a hearse going that way, so I went to church that Sunday, wet and in a hearse with the body not strapped down. So, every time he stopped, the body would bump into the back of my seat. The driver thought he would scare me; I ended up scaring him. The driver said, "Settle down back there. Aren't you afraid?"

Death was very familiar to me, as I had to go with my mother every time someone died. So I said to him, "I'm not afraid of the dead man. I'm afraid of you."

"You're a smart little thing, aren't you?"

I wanted more in life. I knew if I stayed in Memphis, I would end up uneducated and pregnant with the pastor's child. I was so ignorant anyway about reproduction, but little did I know I would, in some ways, pay a heavy price for staying in California, but in other ways, I still believe I made the right choice.

I must admit that in all of my turmoil, I had a good life in Memphis. I was surrounded by a community of people who genuinely cared for one another. My church, school, and family were all a part of it. That shielded me from a lot of the segregation that was part of life in the South. I didn't realize the degree of segregation until I moved away and grew older. It made me appreciate my family and community even more than I did before. I was so insulated that I never thought about being a black girl. I never thought that I couldn't do anything I wanted. I would look at the TV and see the Mouseketeers, and I thought I could be one if only I lived in LA. I never thought about the fact that there were no black girls on the Mouseketeers at that time. That really showed that I was among people who taught me I could be and do anything I wanted. Although that was a large part of who I was in Memphis and who I still am, I always knew and felt there was something bigger outside of that little world of Memphis.

My aunt and uncle drove from California to Memphis. I was so happy to see them and followed them everywhere they went, just in case. I didn't want to get left behind. We finally left in August of 1956. On the way back, they tried to find my oldest brother, so we drove back to California by way of Detroit. I had never seen him before, and I wanted to get to know him. Every time I said this, one of my siblings would say, "He looks just like Papa." I didn't care what he looked like; I wanted to see him for myself. We also tried to find Harry, my boyfriend, who had moved to Detroit. They found my brother's house and saw his wife and kids, but he wasn't there. I don't know why I couldn't go into the house, but they told me to stay in the car. When they said he wasn't there, my heart sank. We didn't find Harry's house either. We later found out that the streets in Detroit run either west or east, or north or south. So, if the house address is on a street and you find that street but not the number, it's because you are on the wrong side of town. I felt we struck out, but the rest of the trip was wonderful. We stopped, ate, and slept in motels at night. All of this was new to me. The scenery was beautiful; my aunt and I sang Via Con Dios all the way to Berkeley. She had a good voice and could harmonize. My uncle did most of the driving. We took Interstate 80, the northern route, because it offered accommodations. The mountains were so majestic. However, the 40 miles of the Great Salt Lake scared me because, although my uncle filled up before we got on it, I somehow thought we would run out of gas. Believe me, on both sides of the road for 40 miles was nothing but salt.

We finally got into Berkeley, and we stopped at a fast-food place called Bobo's. It had this neon sign that went up and popped the balloons at the end of the run. I just knew I had died and gone to heaven.

We drove up to the house, and it looked the same as it did when I visited before. I said to myself, I'm home. Running hot water, an electric washing machine, and a dryer, and I didn't see any little critters or evidence that they were there. I didn't sleep at all that night. The next day, we went grocery shopping, and it just seemed like I was in Neverland. It didn't seem real. We would go to the Tenth Street Market and the Housewives Market. I loved the smell of the roasting peanuts and all the meat hanging. I was like a country bumpkin looking with my mouth open.

We went to church, and I couldn't believe we were out in an hour. We went riding on Sundays, and I must say they took me everywhere. The Golden Gate Bridge was a disappointment at first because I was looking for a golden bridge. I later began to appreciate the span, not the color. Later, I learned that the bridge got its name from the body of water it spans: the strait from the Pacific Ocean into San Francisco Bay, called the Golden Gate Strait. It was named in the 1800s by U.S. Army Captain John C. Fremont, who believed that the strait would become a golden gateway for trade between the United States and Asia. Looks like he was right about that.

As for our summer travels, my disappointment about the bridge didn't last long. We went to Fairyland in Oakland and to Lake Merritt. We went to the Ice Follies. They took me to Yosemite, where I had my first encounter with a bear. We went to the redwoods and drove the car through the trees. This was all so enchanting. I felt like I had died and gone to heaven.

It was getting close to the end of August, and my mom began to ask when they were going to send me home.

I wanted to stay in California. I said, "I am not coming home."

She said, "A disobedient child will not live half its days."

I should have taken that as an omen, but I was too excited to go to Berkeley High. I didn't realize the impact that my staying would have on her. In one way, I regretted it, but in another, I feel I made the right decision for me. I later found out that my mother consulted with a lawyer, who told her that they would have to go to California and arrest me as a runaway and bring me back to Memphis. My mother did not want to suffer that indignity. So, I stayed.

Chapter 8: High School in Berkeley

    My aunt registered me at Berkeley High. I was in the Dean of Girls' Office, where I met my first California friend. Her name was Marie. Her aunt was also registering her, and we later found out that we lived five blocks from each other. My aunt took me to Capwell's basement and bought me two skirts, two tops, shoes, and socks. I didn't really have many clothes because I got only two outfits a year, unless I was in some special program. My aunt Katie would buy most of my clothes, and if I was complimented on them, she said, "Tell them who bought them for you." Never was I allowed to feel special. There was always something or someone to take away the moment. I mainly wore the hand-me-down clothes of my cousin. Unfortunately, she was much larger than I, and I did a lot of pinning because, unlike my grandmother, my mother could not sew. I wanted so badly to work during the summer so I could have new clothes for school, but what the young people had to do, my mother wouldn't let me be a maid, pick cotton, or do any other menial work. But the strange thing is, I don't ever remember anyone saying anything about my clothes. I wanted a sweater because it was cold in California. I wrote to Ed, and he sent me $40 so I could get a sweater and some other things. I didn't know why, but when I got the letter, Aunt Clara told me I had a letter from an Ed in Memphis, and she wanted me to open it and read it in front of her. I thought this was strange and invasive, but I did it anyway. When I opened the letter, two 20-dollar bills fell out. That would be a little more than $400 in today's money.

    She asked, "Who is this man?"

    "He's my boyfriend," I answered.

"How does he have so much money to send you?" as she intruded further.

"Because he works," I replied.

At that, the inquisition ended. I think my mom or Aunt Katie told Aunt Clara that they suspected I had a relationship with the pastor and to be on the lookout for suspicious packages or money. She told me that she would keep the money for me. I was deflated. I asked her if I could get a sweater because I was cold and needed something to keep me warm. Well, she went and bought me a thin coat sweater that I didn't like, and I never saw any of the money. I was in a mess. I couldn't let him send me any more money if she was going to get the mail all the time, and I was going to have to read my letters to her. I wasn't ready for this kind of behavior from her. I later began to think that part of this behavior was that Aunt Clara wanted a baby or a small child. This disappointed her when she realized that I was neither.

She supported me in high school and took me and my friends to all the activities we were doing. She really seemed to enjoy this. The only time she began to bring out the baby thing again was when I won the lead in Babes in Toyland. That was a biggie. It was also the first form of prejudice I experienced at Berkeley. One of the lead male singers had to sing to me, and Ms. Schwimley, the drama teacher, came and told my Aunt that some of the parents did not want him singing to me because he was white and I was black, and he was singing his love for me. Ms. Schwinley was a wonderful teacher. She told my aunt she had thought of a way to get around it by having me flanked by two white girls, and he would sing my dears instead of my dear. Some of my friends were angry when I told them, and they said I shouldn't sing. Well, that was out of the question for me. I had beaten over 200 people for that role, and coming from where I came from, I was not going to give up that kind of opportunity. Anyway, there was so much activity and rehearsals that after the show, my friends wanted to take me out to celebrate, and Aunt Clara decided that I had done enough. My friends had to beg her to let me go. The only other time I experienced this prejudice was while ushering for the Barber Shop Quartet

. When you were part of the drama department, you learned everything about it. You had to do stage, wardrobe, ushering, lighting, and maintenance. I was picked for this event.

My Journey Through Life, Love, and Tragedy

I was at my post in the aisle giving out programs, and this white man came up to me and said, "You didn't give me a program."

I immediately said, "I'm sorry."

He said, "You look sorry."

I was very hurt, but I put on my stage smile and continued to stand my post, passing out programs. I told Ms. Schwinley, and they never sang there as long as I was there. I don't know what happened after I left Berkeley.

I had been told that I was going to really see how a school was run when I got to Berkeley. That they passed classes in an orderly fashion, and I would see how high schoolers really behaved. Well, I found out alright. At Manassas, we passed class in silence. We did not and were not allowed to go to our lockers between passing classes. It was very orderly, I thought, and I often wondered what could be more orderly than that. On the first day at Berkeley, the bell rang, and bedlam broke out. The kids were yelling as they went into their lockers, slamming the doors. And even kissing each other. Of course, I was like a fish out of water because I was expecting just the opposite. I soon got used to that, but one thing I never got used to and hated was swimming. It was a required course at Berkeley. You had to learn a sitting dive, get a magnet off the bottom of the pool, and swim across the pool using any stroke you wanted.

The One Thing I Hated about Berkeley High

Two summers before coming to Berkeley, my mom let me go and spend time with my sister, Marion, in Rockford, Illinois. Her husband had a niece my age, and she allowed us to go swimming. I had never been in a pool before because my mom wouldn't let us go to the colored pools, which were not kept up, and many children were coming down with polio, and she was afraid of water anyway, so all of these things kept me from going to a pool in Memphis. That was not the case in Rockford. Marion was happy to get rid of me so she could have some peace and quiet, so we went to the pool. I was having a great time getting on the slide, coming down, and going back up to do it again and again. Well, this boy thought I wasn't going fast enough, so he pushed me, and when I stood up, there was no floor. Of course, I panicked and began to feel faint and go down. Willie Mae, the niece, was sitting on the side and watching me, thinking I was having a good time, until she didn't see me come up anymore. The next thing I remembered was being on the deck and spitting up water. That was it for me and the swimming pool. When I took my classes at Berkeley, of course, one of them was swimming. This was the only thing I didn't like about going to Berkeley High. I was petrified. The first day of swimming, we all got dressed and went into the pool area. Our teacher came in and told us all to get in the water, and she wanted us to sit under the water, hold our noses, and look until we could hold it no longer. Well, if you ever hold your nose and try to breathe, it gives you the sensation of drowning. I came out of the water screaming. Immediately, she emptied the pool. I was trembling so much I could barely get out. She noticed I was visibly shaken. She had me sit on the bench and directed the others to get back into the pool. She finished the class, but then had me go and get dressed so we could meet in her office. I was still trembling with fear of her now. She asked me what had happened, and I told her about my experience in Rockford. She said she wished my aunt or I had informed her before I went into the pool. She said she would let me work at my own pace and would not grade me down for not being at the point I should be with the class, as long as I tried. The fact that she didn't push me put me somewhat at ease. I was happy I had gotten her because it was rumored that the other teacher would push you off into the deep end and make you swim. I knew if that happened to me, they would have had a casualty on their hands. Because of my teacher's patience and understanding, I finally learned how to do a sitting dive. I could not swim on my face. I could do the back and side stroke. I still did not like swimming, not only because of my experience but also because of my hair. It was always unmanageable. We pressed our hair then, and no matter what you put under your cap, the water would seep underneath. You would come out of the pool looking crazy because one side would be straight and the other side would be bushy. I was so relieved when I finished swimming class. I have never been a sports person.

    I loved Berkeley. There was always something going on. We also had a choice of badminton, volleyball, baseball, track, and dance. My friend and I chose dance. I loved dance. I would be on a dance committee, and we made bids. I had never heard of a bid. This is what you would have filled out by the person who would dance with you. I think they were symbolic because I don't remember anyone having theirs filled out.

    I learned about chairs in band and orchestra. First chair was the best player, and so on. I was never first chair. I excelled in choir. I was a soloist for both the a cappella and Aeolian Choirs. Dr. Blakesley was the director of both. Aunt Clara hired him to teach me privately, and when the other parents found out that I was a soloist, they complained to the office, saying he couldn't teach me privately and publicly. I was still a soloist, and I was a soloist before he started teaching me privately. Dr Blakesley took me all over California and entered me into singing contests. I didn't like some of the songs he wanted me to sing, and I don't think that, as of today, I sing a song that I can't get into or get the feel of it. He thought he knew best, and I believe that's why I always came in second place. Anyway, I loved Dr. Blakesley because he had the guts to make me a soloist, and he was a very good teacher.

At the time I went to Berkeley High, we had an area called the slope. There was a smokestack that divided it. Somehow, the blacks were on one side and the whites on the other. The Mexicans and Orientals were in different areas. We never could have thought we could go over to the white side and vice versa; it was a social thing. We were truly integrated in the classroom, teams, and other activities.

There was one thing that happened that was a first. We had three black girls who became the first black cheerleaders. They won by competing against a lot of teams. They really didn't want them to cheer, and they put two white boys with them. Looking back, the racism was there, but covert instead of overt, like in the South. We also had a voice as blacks; we did not in the South. The strange thing about Berkeley High is that we all still get together, black and white. We celebrated 60 years in 2018. Although we have lost most of our class, the ones that are left are still having fun and remembering old times. There were 587 students in our class. My grandson graduated in 2012, and over a thousand students graduated that year. Berkeley was one of my greatest experiences. I had bumps, but the good outweighed the bad.

Making a Lifelong Friend

I was asked to join a club called the Sophisticates. Two of the members didn't go to Berkeley; they went to Oakland High. When I first went to Berkeley, they had a dance called the Sadie Hawkins dance. That's where the girls ask the boys to dance, instead of the traditional practice of boys asking the girls. I asked this young man, and I thought we were an item until I learned through the club that he was also going with this girl from Oakland High. It came to a head when one of the members had a party and invited all of us. Everyone began to say it's going to be a fight. I knew I wasn't going to fight, and especially not over a boy.

That was one thing my mother wouldn't allow, and it just hurts me to see these girls today not think of themselves enough to know not to fight over a boy. My mother said, "You are the prize. If anybody is going to fight, let them fight over you."

I didn't know what the other girl thought, but we ended up at this party. I got there first, and then here comes Pat with her posse. She always travelled with a posse. Everybody was sure we would fight. She came up to me and asked if I would come outside. Well, that was an indication it was on. So, I go outside, and everybody is crowded at the door to see.

"My name is Pat," she said.
"My name is Cora," I replied.
"How serious are you about this boy?" she asked.
"How serious are you?" I responded.
"I can take him or leave him," she said.
"I feel the same."
So, she said, "Let's forget him and be friends."

We have not only been friends for over 50 years, but she has also become my sister-in-law. And we have gone and done almost everything together.

When I graduated from Berkeley High, my mother sent me three dresses from Robinsons store. It was a type of store like Walmart. I was very impressed because of all my accomplishments, but she never said she was proud of me. I heard she had published it in the school paper, 'Memphis Girl Makes Good,' and wrote about my accomplishments, but I was never notified. You may be wondering where my father was. He was there in body but not in any other way. He resented having another mouth to feed. I heard he was very upset with my mother sending me the dresses. I think it was a combination of age and tiredness, and I don't think he believed I was his. When I talked to my other siblings about him, they looked at me like I was crazy because they all had a different relationship with him. They could tell me all the things they did when they were coming up. He made my oldest sister a dollhouse and all the furniture for it. He played pitty pat cards with my sisters, brothers, and nephew Bubba, but he never said anything to me. No hugs, no nothing. I began to discount him and no longer thought of him as my father. When I hear others speak of their fathers in terms of endearment, I often wonder, "How does that feel?" I will get into him in my other book.

Back to Church
One day, my aunt stated, "You have to join a church."
"I want to join St. Joseph's," I said as I recalled my memories.
When I was 12, I would go to Chicago every other summer to visit my cousin. The other summers, my cousin would come to Memphis. They were Catholic. When I walked into their church, I was awed by all the pageantry and incense. After the service was over in 45 minutes, I told my mother, 'I want to become Catholic.'
She said, 'Absolutely not. Methodist is the only true church.' I guess she had told this to my aunt.

"Your mother doesn't want you to become Catholic, but you have to join a church," my aunt insisted. Instead of telling me I had to join South Berkeley, she went all around the bush. I joined South Berkeley, and of course, I joined the choir. They sang anthems instead of gospel and hymns. They even had Leontyne Price to sing one Sunday. I was in the young people's group, and my aunt and uncle were in charge of it. We did a lot of activities. We went to the beach and went camping. One time we went to the ocean, and I didn't have a swimsuit. I was wearing a pair of shorts and a top made entirely of elastic. I went down into the water, and when I came up, everyone was laughing and pointing because my top had come down and my breasts were completely exposed. I just pulled it up and didn't give them a chance to make me feel bad. The Congregational church had a beautiful campground. I remember going to camp one summer, and if you put your elbows on the table, they would all sing, "Whoever had their elbows on the table, strong and able, take your elbows off the table; round the barn you must go." We also made up plays, and there was a student from Berkeley High named Robin, and she and I hit it off, so we decided to do Little Red Robin Hood. I suppose it was because she had red hair that we came up with this. We were the hit of the camp. Every time we saw each other at school and in my yearbook, she would sign Wolfie. It was funny because we switched the roles; I played Little Red Riding Hood, and she was the wolf.

I met Rickey, whom I call that, although it was not his real name. However, in respect for his children, I will not disclose his real name. He sang in the choir at South Berkeley. He looked and sounded like Billy

Ekstine. Although he was much older than I, we found each other attractive. Before he came into my life, I had many boyfriends.

Meeting Huey Newton

The famous Huey Newton transferred to Berkeley, and he was fine, as we always said. So of course, I went up to him to welcome him to Berkeley, and we got to talking, and we ended up making a date to go to the movie on the weekend. On the way to my house, when he got off the bus, he was attacked by some Berkeley boys. When he got to my house, he was angry and in no mood to do anything but exact revenge. My aunt sat him on the toilet and put medicine on his wounds, and he left, promising me he would take me to a dance the following week. Well, he came to school that Monday to find and do damage to the boys who had attacked him. Somehow, someone found out, and he was brought to the office and relieved of his weapons. After reviewing his file, it was discovered that he had given an aunt's address, and they quickly sent him back to his old school. The following week came, and he was true to his word; a gentleman came. When I opened the door, there stood his brother. He didn't come to take me. Needless to say, we didn't go to the dance. I was too disappointed and confused. Most boys would not have given me a second thought, but because he wouldn't or couldn't come, he provided me with a date. I never would have guessed anything like what became his future at that time. He was brilliant and started the Black Panthers. Unfortunately, he was not appreciated until later in his life, and his life was more than some people could have ever imagined.

I was having fun. Believe it or not, Pat and I went out with the same boy we were to fight over. We would go to a drive-in called Hokies. They sold these butter burgers. They were a heart attack ready to happen. However, I suppose we were so active at that time that we weren't affected. At that time, I didn't have a weight problem; Pat did, but because her mother made all her clothes, she hid a lot of it.

Our ex-boyfriend had an old Ford that was lowered in the front. That was the thing then, to lower your car. The Mexicans would put their cars on hydraulics and, at the stop signs, raise and lower their cars up and down. We called them the low riders. Pat and I did everything together. Considering how we met, it was amazing that we were so compatible. She was going to be a debutante, and she told me to come on and be one so we could be together. We found out you had to be sponsored by a Link organization giving the ball. One of the most prominent Link members belonged to South Berkeley, so I asked her if she would sponsor me, and she said she would be honored. We had parties, pictures taken, we were featured in the newspaper, we had teas - you name it. It was a good experience and I had fun, but when I was looking for a job, I wondered where that connection was that this type of affair would help you get one.

One of my most fond memories was when we were initiated into the choir. It had been said that it was really scary and people would faint with fear. The day came, and all the new members were in the choir room waiting for their fate. We were led out one by one. We could hear the hollering, and that made it all the worse. When they came to get me, of course, the closer I got to the door, the louder I began to holler. I was pulling back so hard, but when the door opened, so did my mouth. In the Green room, all of the choir members were there singing *No Man Is an Island* and each one had the new member's robe. They put the robe on you and gave you a candle. It was the most moving experience.

When we graduated from Berkeley, my friend Marie and I were slated to go to San Francisco State. I was so excited about graduating that I was in a euphoric state. My vocal cords collapsed. So, I was mouthing all the songs the choir sang. I was disappointed not to be able to sing the benediction. I cried because I knew this was a part of my life I would never live again. I knew we would never all be together again.

One of my classmates' mothers bought her a brand-new car as a graduation gift. You can't believe how excited we all were. I think about the culture of kids today and how they would likely react. They would have probably been jealous. But we were all so excited for her. I was speechless to see a black kid get a new car. We all crowded around, and she took us in batches around the block. It was just a glorious time. We all went our separate ways, but we kept in contact through conversation and by seeing each other in stores and other places we visited. We still get together today, the ones that are left. We truly bonded.

Part 5

A Dark Family Secret

Chapter 9: Life After High School

I went and took the placement test for San Francisco State. I thought Marie went back to Louisiana for the summer. But when she didn't return to take the test with me, I asked her aunt, and she said Marie was not coming back. I think this set me up for failure. I can't blame it all on her, but it diminished my drive to go to San Francisco State. I felt I had lost a family member. I felt we were sisters. We both came from the south, and because we didn't attend grammar and middle school there, to some, we were outsiders. They used to say they were California girls.

I took the test, and to my surprise, I ended up having to take an English lab. I thought I would have to take a math lab. I began to feel more a part after my aunt paid for me to go to Frosh camp. I met other freshmen, and I was a part of the group. Little did I know I was not part of anything. Before I began college, Pat and I did everything that summer. We went to Los Angeles to visit my sister and go to Disneyland. Disneyland was always available to us, even after I had children, because my brother-in-law played bass in Teddy Buckner's Dixie Land Jazz Band in the New Orleans sector. We were privileged to go in through the family door, so we took advantage of this any time we could. Pat and I drove down in her Renault car. We had it loaded with teddy bears, Mickey Mouses, and all kinds of toys we were going to put in our room at home.

On the way back, we had just exited the six-mile portion of Interstate 5 in Kern County, known as the Grapevine, when I couldn't get the car out of the gear it was in. I tried several times, and we decided we should pull over. The problem was that we were in the middle of nowhere. It was a little town called Pixley. We sat and thought about what we could do. No phone, of course. We looked over the field and saw a house. We thought if we could get to it, maybe they had a phone. Well, we started, and the dogs began to bark, and I began to get scared. I think Pat was, too. When we found ourselves in a predicament, as we often did, she would say, "Well, you know we've had a good life, but this may be it." We finally reached this house, and I thought I had been transported in time back to the country in Memphis. They had a well and a bucket with a dipper in it. They were white hillbillies, and I guess God was looking out for us because they went and towed the car back to their yard and began to call around for a timing gear. They had decided this was the problem. It was promised to come on the next bus at 4 o'clock. It didn't come on the 4 o'clock bus, and it didn't come on the next one or the next one after that. It was getting dark, and I was dirty and thirsty and didn't want to drink out of the dipper. Pat said you better not, but I had to, and I did, as we had done before, threw out what you didn't drink. They took us to the highway with as much as we could carry and put us on the bus to Oakland. They called Pat's father, and he met us there. He went down two days later and brought the car home. We had many other experiences together. It seemed we attracted trouble. One day, we had stopped at the light, and before it could turn green, this man behind us blew his horn, and Pat, without knowing what the other was doing, gave him the finger. He began to follow us, and again Pat said, "Well, we have had a good life; this may be it."

    He followed us to Pat's house, and Pat parked the car on the wrong side of the street, which allowed her to get out, leaving me facing this guy. She ran into the house to get her father and was talking to him out of the door while I was trying to disappear.

    Pat said something to him, and he responded, saying, "That's just the reason we don't want you people up here with us."

    She said, "Well, we are ha ha."

    Of course, she also called him a racist pig, and I was so glad when he drove off so I could get out of the car. I told her thanks when I got into the house. I would hate to think of what would have happened in these times.

    Summer was over, and it was time to go to San Francisco State. College was truly out of my league. First, my aunt had to pay out-of-state fees for me. Secondly, I was not ready for a 4-year college. I had managed to get through school relatively easily, thanks to a lot of help and guidance. I found out I was on my own, and the year I registered, the system they set up meant the freshmen registered last. No classes available. No counselors to talk to. They were all too busy with other students. I wandered around until I got an English class at four in the afternoon, a psychology class at 11:00 a.m., and an English lab at 9:00 a.m. on Monday. Wednesday was an elective that I can't remember now. I never attended school at 4 in the evening. The English class was discussing books I had never heard of, and there seemed to be special relationships with some of the students. Again, I felt like a fish out of water. The only class I truly enjoyed was psychology. I tried discussing it with my aunt, and she said, "Don't talk to me about that. And don't try to analyze me."

Because of my lack of discipline, I spent time in the student union learning to play bid whist. My mother didn't allow us to play cards at home because she said that when she met my father, he used to be a gambler. I was also having fun with the Alpha men and partying. They kept my name in the paper, threatening me to leave this one Alpha alone, or they wouldn't let me be an AKA. Well, anyone who knows me would realize that just meant I wouldn't. I didn't really want to be in a sorority anyway because they had blackballed one of my classmates from Berkeley High, and I have never wanted to be in any group that discriminated based on personalities. The sororities and fraternities were supposed to be based on your scholarship and not your color or your economic status. I tried to study, and we attempted to form study groups, but we would often end up having fun at Cal's library instead. I truly lost any focus or discipline I should have had. For the first time, I felt free of everything and threw caution to the wind.

My grandfather passed away while I was at San Francisco State. I went home like a peacock because I was at San Francisco State, and most of my Memphis friends were at local colleges. Because they all became successful and had great jobs, and I, in turn, ended up not graduating, I felt I really was not the peacock I thought I was. I flunked out of San Francisco State. They would not allow me back into school. They said I could take summer classes and appeal to return. This really woke me up, and I took two classes, earning an A in one and a B in the other. However, they thought I needed a more structured school environment.

The leap from high school to a 4-year school was overwhelming. Plus, it was expensive to pay out-of-state fees. I registered at Oakland City College, which later became Merritt. I scheduled the classes at times that were like high school, plus a lot of my friends from Berkeley were there. It was challenging but manageable, and I was enjoying myself again. As they say, all good things come to an end.

Chapter 10: Confrontation & Exile

One night, my aunt asked me to go and get my uncle from the barber shop to eat and bring her something back. I thought nothing of this, but later I found out she was setting me up because she had a suspicion that my uncle wanted me, and of course, if this was true, it was because I had enticed him. To this day, this is still mind-boggling to me.

We went to dinner, and while talking, he began by saying, "You shouldn't have come out here."

Now I'm really confused because he was the one who told everybody to leave us alone. I asked, "What are you talking about?"

He didn't answer my question, but said, "It's too late now because we were going to this hotel."

"For what?" I questioned.

He said, "You know what."

Confused, I said, "No, I don't. Are you meeting someone there?"

He just looked at me. I ran out so that I could drive, because if I drove, I would have control, and secondly, he had been drinking as usual. When he got into the car, he began touching me.

"Stop! You're my uncle," I told him.

He said, "I'm not your blood uncle."

"I don't care, and if you don't stop touching me, I'm going to wreck the car," I threatened.

He mused, "You let the other boys do it."

I can't describe what or how I was feeling. But my mother came to me, and I began to understand why this was one of the reasons she didn't want me to come to California. I will go into the history of this in my sequel. He threatened me when he realized I was almost home and said, "We're going to do it, and you better not tell your aunt."

I was shaking when I got home, took a shower, and went to bed. I was so confused about what to do. I asked my friends at school, and they advised me to tell my aunt. I thought I didn't have any other choice. Because my aunt went to work before I went to school, and before he went to work, I thought he would try to overpower me and rape me. So, I decided to tell my aunt. What did I do that for?

The first thing out of her mouth was "I have been trying to keep you two apart."

Now I feel like I have gone mad and am in the snake pit. "Keep us apart! What are you talking about?" I shouted. No answer.

From then on, I became the enemy of my aunt's state. If I was sitting in my room, the kitchen was right outside, she would come and close the door. Was this the disobedient child my mom is talking about? I felt I was the only person on earth. I had taken the advice from my friends, and look what happened. I couldn't call anybody in Memphis. I was all alone.

This all came to a head on New Year's Day. I went to a party on New Year's Eve and was told by my aunt to be home at midnight. I tried to protest, but I was told either be home by midnight or I couldn't go. I went, and we were having so much fun. The biggest event on New Year's Eve is midnight, when the new year comes in. I called the house to plead again, but no one answered. We stayed and had wine at midnight and immediately headed for the bridge. I got home at 12:20 am. At that time, I would enter through the back door. It was always unlocked. Rickey and I stood and kissed and necked, and he left, and I went in and went to bed. The next day, I got up and warmed up some leftover food. I got my books out to study for finals. My aunt came home ready for a fight. I guess the thing between me and her husband had reached a boiling point.

She came in for lunch and immediately asked me, "What time did you get home?"

"I was 20 minutes late. I got home at 12:20," I told her.

"I looked at my clock and it was 2:00," she ranted.

"I was 20 minutes late. I got home at 12:20," I repeated.

She said, "You are so ungrateful. You knew I was coming home for lunch, and you didn't fix anything for me."

"When I used to fix you lunch, you would tell me you wished I didn't fix that because you were going to have that for dinner," I explained. "You can have what I have warmed up," I continued.

"I don't want that mess!" she shouted.

I went to sit down, but before I could sit down, she came up and said, "I'm tired of you lying to me."

She backhanded me and cut my face with her ring. In all the whipping I received, neither my mother nor anyone else ever hit me in my face. I saw everything under the sun. I went up to her and slapped her, and her glasses flew off and hit the doorknob.

She said, "You broke my glasses!" as she began to choke me.

I was really losing breath, and I began to pull her hair until she got off of me. She unleashed all of her anger on me. I can't describe the feeling. All I knew was that my feelings for her had vanished, and she looked like someone I had never known. She turned and told me, "Get out of my house!"

"I'll get out after I get a call from Rick," I told her.

"You better not be here when I come back!" she demanded.

I was trembling with fear and uncertainty. While I was trying to figure out what to do, my aunt had gotten on the phone to my uncle and all the people in Memphis. The story she told was that I had hit her, broken her glasses, and was running amok. I had enticed the uncle. In the meantime, I was trying to find a place to stay. My brother and his family lived only four blocks away, and I called to see if I could come and stay with them. I told him I had to get out of Aunt Clara's house. He said he would talk it over with his wife. I asked if I could just come and spend the night because I had no place to go. He said I guess so.

He never asked, "What happened? Are you alright? Do I need to come and get you?" Nothing but, "I guess so."

It dawned on me I had no one in California but these people, and they did not want me around them. I never got a call from my mom to hear my side of the story. How can a person constantly be hurt due to no fault of their own? What had I done? I didn't know until later that I was accused of enticing my uncle. That was another spear in my heart. If he had been the last man on earth, I would not have looked at him, much less have had a relationship with him. He was an alcoholic and abusive, and I knew I would never have a relationship with anyone like that. But as I look back, I began to notice the things he did when my male friends came over. He would embarrass them, saying, 'Can't you speak?' Well, when they came in, he looked like he was asleep. I never knew anyone to wake someone up out of sleep to speak. He really broke me up with one of the guys I truly loved because he was timid and afraid to come over because of my uncle. But it never dawned on me he was doing this for his own benefit. I later found out from people at the barber shop that he would talk about me as if I were his and make up stories about us, and they were not to say anything to me.

Anyway, Rickey said he would call me on his lunch break, and he did. When he called, the dam broke. It was several minutes before I could compose myself to tell him what happened. He said to calm down, and he would come over to my brother's house after work. So, I packed my schoolbooks, some clothes, and enough to carry, and went to my brother's house. When I got there, they were gone. I walked to the back and sat on their porch until they came back. They finally let me in, and again, what happened? No nothing. I sat on the sofa, and the phone began to ring. My sister-in-law said it was Uncle Horace.

She gave me the phone, and he said, "I'm coming over there and blow your brains out. You hit my wife and broke her glasses."

I handed the phone back. I prayed for Rickey to get there before he did. He was the only person I felt could and would protect me. Rickey finally got there and introduced himself to my brother. I told him about the threat, and he asked my brother if he would be home. My brother said he had to go to work. Rickey asked if he could take me to one of his friends' houses until tomorrow, and maybe Uncle Horace would have cooled down by then. He also felt he wouldn't do anything to his family; it was just me he was angry with. After my brother not picking me up, after not asking me anything, he all of a sudden was reluctant to let me go with Rickey. Rickey assured him where I would be and gave him the phone number. Rickey took me to this lady's house, everybody called Mom. I can say that God finally provided me with someone who cared enough to listen to me and give me advice. She became my Godsend. The next morning, I called my sister-in-law, and that is when she told me everything Uncle Horace had done with my clothes. They had come in the night and thrown everything I ever had in the street in front of my brother's house. My sister-in-law and a neighbor brought them inside and piled them in the middle of the floor. Some of my dresses were torn where he had stepped on them. My aunt was packing my things, and he threw them. The most shocking thing after seeing my clothing and other articles of mine was the announcement that they were sending me to Los Angeles to my oldest sister. I was told they had discussed it and agreed that I should go to Los

Angeles. My school, my desires, and my wants were never taken into consideration. I was to go to LA because I needed a job, and my sister assured them she could get me a job where she worked. I was to leave that night. Not a word from Memphis. Not what happened? Are you alright? Do you want to come home? I never thought I would hear 'I love you.' Of all the questions, that is one I would never hear.

Rickey came, and I told him what they had decided. He said, "You don't have to go, I'll take care of you." I don't know why I wasn't comfortable with that at the time. I thought about my school, but I would not have passed my finals. Too much had happened, and I didn't study and wasn't in the frame of mind to study. I was like a jigsaw puzzle riding on a roller coaster, shaking the pieces up even more. I told him I would go and work and save my money to come back. He gave me $100.00, more money than I had ever had, and that was mine. He also said he would come and get me anytime. Those were the most reassuring words I had heard in months.

As I stated earlier, I cried all the way to LA. I really felt hollow inside. I never thought coming to California and experiencing all the wonderful things I had done and achieved would turn out to be me being on a bus with my teddy bear going to a place I never liked. I never liked Los Angeles. I still don't today.

After arriving, the first thing out of LaRaine's mouth was "You really did it this time."

To this day, I can't understand why no one asked me for my side of the story. It was all Aunt Clara and what she had told everybody. Why wasn't I considered a person? Why was everything said about me believed? What had I done? What behavior had I exhibited that caused me not to be believed or have a voice in something that involved me? Did anybody realize there are two sides to every story, no matter which one you believe? Anyway, she said I was to stay with her neighbor, who lived in a little duplex behind the house next door. He lived with his girlfriend. He was an ex-fighter and a little punch-drunk. She was much older than he, but I guess they had a relationship. From the time I got there, she never introduced herself. She would come to the door and ask questions of Carl, but go back into the bedroom. I wondered why I couldn't stay with LaRaine? I later found out my reputation had preceded me, and LaRaine's husband said I couldn't stay there because I had attacked Aunt Clara. I was treated like a specimen sitting on Carl's sofa. His friends came one by one, saying, "Is that Lo's sister? Man, she is fine."

They didn't realize there was a 20-year difference between us because LaRaine was beautiful when she was younger. She didn't look that bad to me, but 20 years is 20 years. Later that night, after I asked for bedding, Carl told me I would sleep in the bed and he would sleep on the sofa. His girlfriend came out and said, "I'll be damned." I don't sleep with women, and I accused him of wanting to get in my pants since I arrived. They got into it so bad that he ended up getting into a fight, and she left. The first house she went to was LaRaine's, and of course, again I am the culprit. She came running over to Carl's and began by saying, "You can't go anywhere without causing trouble. Just be ready in the morning so I can take you to Gold's department store."

She picked me up right at the time she said she would, and I was completely exhausted and struggling to understand what had happened just three days ago.

She had already talked to management about me working there, and after introductions, they found a desk and proceeded to show me what I was to do. I was a credit checker. I was privileged to have people's personal information. At first, it was interesting and a distraction from my predicament. It was only after work that I began to miss school, my friends, and Ricky. I couldn't take it after two weeks. I got so bored, and no one to talk to but Carl. By the way, he called me Little Sport. He was the sweetest guy and tried everything to make me happy. My sister had a nickname for everybody, and his was watermelon seed eyes because his eyes were close together, but I would have never thought of that name.

I called Ricky and asked him if he could come and get me. He said it would be another two weeks before he could come, and I was disappointed, but it was something to look forward to. I never told LaRaine because I didn't want to hear the backlash. The week went as usual, and Saturday morning, LaRaine called me to come over. I had a phone call. The voice said, "Do you want to go to breakfast?"

I screamed, "Ricky, where are you?"

"I am at the corner," he said, calling from a pay phone down the street. "I will be there as soon as I can turn around," he answered.

By the time I got to the front door, he was pulling up with a friend in the car. I flew into his arms and cried. I was so happy. He came inside, and I introduced him to LaRaine. I also announced I was going back to

Berkeley. She pulled me into the room to tell me, "The Pastor (my Ed from Memphis) is in LA, and you have to go and see him before you go back."

"I am not going to see him," I told her.

"He promised Mama that he would see and talk to you," she told me.

I guess he thought he could talk me into going home. Ricky said I should go. Ricky knew all about him, and I think he wanted to see this man. We went to see him, and I introduced them.

"May I talk to Cora alone?" he asked.

"I don't mind," Ricky answered.

He comes up to me, kisses me, and tells me,

> "I miss you so much! Won't you come back to Memphis? It would mean the world to me, but most of all, it would please your mother. She really needs you home.
>
> "I'll see that we move into a more suitable house. I'll buy you a car, and you can go to LeMoyne to finish college."

It all sounded attractive, but the price was too high. I really didn't want to go with the pastor of the church and be dependent on his whims and wants. What if they sent him to another church? Then, where would I be? I also thought of my mama, who had been and was still silent. She still hadn't said anything to me, and now she was speaking through this person who really didn't care about her interests but his own. He left me with the option that if I change my mind, I could always call him.

Part 6

My Struggle for Stability

Chapter 11: A New Beginning in Oakland

Ricky and I left, and I never looked back. We had a wonderful ride home. We took our time, stopping to shop and eat at wonderful restaurants. When we finally got back to Oakland, he took me to Mom's. I settled in and slept a peaceful sleep that I hadn't had in a long time. I lost all of my classes at Oakland City and would have to take them over if I returned. I began looking for a job and found one as a telemarketer. There were two of us, a blond girl and I, and we were on trial. I out-sold her 3 to 1, but at the end of the day, they kept her and let me go.

I talked to my friend Pat. "I feel so defeated because I can't get a job," I said, feeling sorry for myself. "You know, we were at the debutante ball, and we were supposed to be presented to society, which would put us in a position to get a good job or a husband. I don't see either one."

"My mother told me to go to the Urban League, where they were hiring people for the company," she shared.

I went the next day, and they sent me to the phone company, and I was scheduled for a test to be a telephone representative. I went the next week and took the test. They said they couldn't tell us how long it would be to process the test and application, but they would be in contact. Three weeks passed, and I hadn't heard from them. In the meantime, LaRaine is calling me to come back so that I can have my job back. I talked to Ricky about it, and he said he would support my decision, but he really didn't want me to go. I was getting sick with a cold. I wasn't eating right, and I was already underweight. I waited another week, and then I called the phone company to see if they could at least tell me if I passed the test and if there was any possibility of me being called. They said they couldn't tell anything at that time. I left the next day for LA. Again, Ricky said he would come and get me if I couldn't take it. I told him I was really going to try and make a go of it, but I really wanted him to come and see me as often as possible. I truly loved and depended on him.

I arrived in LA that evening, and LaRaine had gotten me a room across the street from her with this really weird lady and a crazy looking house. I thought I had landed in the little house of horrors. She was really weird. The next day, I went over to LaRaine's, and Art was there. We got to talking, and for once, I was able to tell my side of the story. I told him why I hit Aunt Clara, and I had never disrespected her before, but she was accusing me of something I didn't do, plus she cut my face and slapped me first. I was surprised he was sympathetic to my story. He told LaRaine I could move into the house. Somehow Carl found out I was back, and he told me to come back to his house and get out of that crazy woman's house. I went back to Carl's. He was my bud, and he adored me. He would go and buy me anything I wanted to eat or wear. He also let me drive his car to work, which really irked LaRaine. She wanted me to be dependent on her so she could control the time we left for work. She didn't like me to be independent. I was also sick and found out I had pneumonia. I couldn't work for a week and a half. When I did go back, it was as if I never left. I stayed a total of a month. I think I may have stayed longer, but again LaRaine accused me of trying to get her fired. Everybody ate at one of two places: the drugstore across the street with a lunch counter in it, or the Jewish Deli up the street, behind the store. I loved the Jewish deli. They had the best pastrami I had ever eaten.

One day, the young white guy who worked there came by my desk and said he heard I liked the Jewish Deli, and would I like to go to lunch with him. I told him yes. The next day, we went to the deli, and we talked about everything except who he was, which at the time didn't mean anything to me. He was just another guy who was nice enough to treat me to lunch.

When I got home, she lit into me. "Do you know who you went to lunch with today?" she pried.

I said, "No, just the guy I see around working in different departments."

"That is Mr. Gold's son, the owner. Are you trying to get me fired?" she asked.

"How is going to lunch with someone who asked me is going to get you fired?" I said, puzzled by her intense attack.

My Journey Through Life, Love, and Tragedy

"You just don't know what you are doing. You are playing out of your league, and you will not go to lunch with him again, do you understand me?" she said emphatically.

I really couldn't answer because I, for the first time, began to doubt my thinking. *Do I think like so-called normal people, or am I mentally challenged? Things hadn't made sense since I told Aunt Clara about her husband. My thinking is, if I had wanted him, why would I tell her? But maybe normal people think differently. I really began to question my sanity for the first time. Are my values all wrong? Am I really being punished like I was told I would? Is God angry with me? Is there a lesson in this that I am not learning? It is said that God allows you to go through troubled times so that you can learn a lesson. I am questioning myself now. What is my lesson? My disobedience? My having an affair with an older man? What?*

Again, I called Ricky and told him I was coming home for good this time. He told me to be sure because he couldn't keep coming to get me. I needed to get settled and try to sort this out. I agreed. He came at the end of the week. I informed LaRaine I was leaving for good, and please don't ask me to come back. I felt she had accused me of trying to get her fired from her job. She had accused me of Carl and his girlfriend breaking up. She accused me of making trouble everywhere I went. She never asked me what happened. She never asked me how I felt. She never knew the tears I had shed, nor had she seemed to care. I thanked her for getting me the job at Golds, and I packed my clothes and left for good. I decided if I had to beg on the streets, I would never come back to LA.

Ricky and I left, and on the way home, he said he didn't know how to tell me, but he felt he had to. She called him into the room to talk to him, and I never gave it a thought. I thought she was complaining about me, but she propositioned him. She asked him if he was tired of me because I was so much younger, and that he needed a mature woman like her. I asked him what she said. He said I turned and came out of the room as fast as I could, and we are here together. I just couldn't believe it. But I knew Ricky had no reason to lie to me, and I knew he was not in the room long enough to do anything with her. I knew he was in a hurry when he came out and grabbed me, literally pulling me out the door. Again, my disbelief in my family and family members.

We again rode back to Oakland, and again I settled at Mom's. I called the phone company and was told that they had called me the day I left to set up an interview. They also said I scored the highest in all the ones tested that day, and now I would have to be put back into the queue. I can't begin to tell you at this point what I felt. Was the whole world against me? I waited every day for a call. I would go somewhere and check with Mom to see if anyone had called. About two weeks later, I received a call from the phone company informing me that all the service representatives' jobs were filled. But they had openings as a telephone operator, and asked if I would be interested. I said most definitely. They asked if I could come in that next Thursday at 2:00 pm for an interview. I said I could. Mom and I just shouted, and I got so excited. I then began to go through the little clothes I had left and decided on a green checked suit. I had on heels and white gloves. Little did I know that the gloves got me the job. She said that I could start on Monday at 8:00 am, and not to be late. She stressed that punctuality and attendance were very important. I would be making 60 dollars a week. I thought that was more than my father did after working more than 30 years in a saw mill. They hired a lot of black girls all at once, and we had to pull straws for seniority. I didn't care about anything except that I had a job. It seemed that the job also caused the difference in age to be a factor in Ricky's problems. For the first time, we began to differ in a lot of things. It wasn't because of the money I was making; it was the social life. All the girls would go out, and he was a cog in the wheel. We also went out on dates, and he didn't feel comfortable because the places catered to younger people. I really loved Ricky, but I also loved the life of the phone company. I also found out that he began to date the lady he was seeing before we got together. We grew apart without us knowing we were growing apart.

NO! I'm Not Going Back
The pastor came out during this time. He was at the St. Francis Hotel in San Francisco. He asked if I could come over. I told him I would have to have someone bring me. My girlfriend, who was the union steward, said she could take me but couldn't bring me back. I called and told him, and he said he would pay her and then send me home in a car. She took me over, and he wanted sex. I told him, "No." One, I didn't want to, and second, it was that time of the month. Again, he started about me coming home. He didn't put my mother into the conversation this time. It was him and him alone that needed me to come home. I tried to tell him I was happy with my life here in California. What future did I have in

My Journey Through Life, Love, and Tragedy

Memphis? He said again, this time he would buy me a house, and I could wait until he bought it and put it in my name if I didn't trust him. He would also buy me a car and anything else I wanted. Clothes, shoes, just anything I wanted. I asked him why he would do this. Was it sex, love, or ego? He said it was a little of all of it. He loved my spirit, and I was not like anyone else he had met. I asked him about his wife and children. He said they would not suffer behind this. I asked him, "What about your soul? You think God will forgive you, knowing what you know?" He couldn't answer that. I told him at the time he paid attention to me, I was a little girl who needed someone to show me love and attention. I was also captive to having to go to church. I told him I was not that little girl anymore, and no matter what material things he offered, they would not bring back the magic of the little girl that he had tried to take her virginity. I kind of felt sorry for him because of the sadness in his eyes. I could see that he really understood that it was over, and I was not coming back to Memphis. He ordered a limousine to take me home.

    I soon began to get involved in the politics of the phone company. My friend was a union steward, and she informed me of a lot of things I really didn't like. For some reason, I can't stand injustice. I guess I had had enough of it, and I just couldn't keep my mouth shut when I knew it was wrong. They wouldn't let the black girls sit together. They said we had a conspiracy against the phone company, and of course, I was the ringleader. They wouldn't let us wear pants. It would be so cold and rainy sometimes, and we had to wear dresses, heels, and stockings. I asked why we couldn't wear pants. They said that because the men wanted to see our legs. I said that was sexist. The white women got the best shift because it was supposedly based on seniority. They worked six hours and got paid for eight. We had to work broken shifts and never got the holidays off. People were coming in and working six months and being transferred to offices that worked 9 to 5. Some of us started a social club. We had a formal dance and a sweetheart who later became my boyfriend. We really had fun as a group. When I had made enough money, I got an apartment with this lady. It was one bedroom, but we had twin beds. She was to furnish the bedroom, and I was to furnish the living room. I went to this furniture store that sold futuristic furniture, and we had a beautiful living room. After I thought about it, she got the best deal because all she bought were beds. She had a son by some famous artist, and he would stay with her or his family, and some weekends he would stay with us. She was quirky, that's how I can describe her. One day, she wanted me to scratch her head, and I did, only to run into all these threads and braids. I asked her what this was, and she said I have a weave. I asked her what a weave was. She told me it was where they sewed hair onto your hair. I always admired her hair; it was long and beautiful, but it was a long time before the general public began to get weaves. Now it is a common thing for people to have weaves. Ricky and I were seeing each other less and less, but we would meet at Mom's and get together. I still had feelings for him. Mom pulled my coat, saying, "Don't give up everything for him, because he was seeing the woman before we got together." Mom said, "You are a young baby, and you have to play it while you can."

Mom was the most beautiful lady I've ever met. She was Creole, and I can imagine her when she was younger; she was even more gorgeous.

I tried to make up for all the clothes I didn't have growing up by buying everything I saw and wanted. I regretted not saving more and sending my mom some money. I would sometimes spend my bus fare home, and had to go back to the phone company and borrow money from our second mom. She was the matron and was so proud of us. Unlike the cafeteria workers who acted like they couldn't stand us, Minnie was proud we had come up and was an operator. She helped all of us out. She would cook for us, and she called her husband Sweetheart. She helped one of the operators buy a car. One time, my friend and I went to her house for dinner, and she told us what had happened to her while she was waiting for her sweetheart to pick her up. She said,

"Cora, I went to the bank, and there was no place to park, so Sweetheart drove around until I came out. When I came out, this man came up to me and said, 'Where did the 40 bus drop you off?'

"I didn't know because I didn't ride the bus," I said.

He said, 'Ah, you know you just don't want to tell me.'

Irritated, I said, "Sir, I am waiting for my husband to pick me up." He said to me, 'Husband, somebody as ugly as you has a husband?'

Well, it took the police and Sweetheart to get me off of him. My friend laughed so hard I thought I was going to have to take her to the hospital. She couldn't get her breath.

Minnie was another sweet person God put in my life, and I will always feel warm when I think of her. We all knew we could depend on her for loans. She would fuss, but she would always say You girls look so good. One of the other memorable moments was when President Kennedy was shot. The board lit up all over the room. We were trained to pick up a signal as quickly as possible because we never knew if it was an emergency. The supervisors and everybody were working. If there was an empty board next to you, we worked that one too. We had no time to pull the key back to hear the conversation, and when it began to die down, one of the supervisors came down with a sign that said President Kennedy was dead. Pandemonium broke out. People were crying and still having to take calls. Some had to be excused. It was kind of everyone to be in the seat of communication and be the last to know what was going on.

Chapter 12: Love & Loss in San Francisco

I was invited to a 4th of July party. My Memphis friend was friends with the lady hosting it, and though she couldn't go, for some reason, she wanted me to go. I was so happy I did because I met a very fascinating man who had just graduated from Law school and was drinking and celebrating like mad. He was so fine. We hit it off and left the party and went to Strawberry Creek and a building on Cal's campus. We get there, and people are streaming out. He asked what was going on. Someone said the fire department is closing it down because there are too many people. He said, "Baby, we're going in here, and if we get separated, meet me at the car." I said, 'Okay.' So we sneak in one of the offside doors, and there were still a lot of people there. Everybody was congratulating him on finishing law school and making fun of him. They had a case for him already. We are holding hands in the middle of the floor, and suddenly someone comes and breaks us apart. Well, I'm looking around, and he is totally lost in the crowd. I turned and looked in the direction of the main door, and near there was a little rise that looked like it was the band or speaker platform. Two guys were standing on the platform. One of them looked like Harry. I stood there and tried to collect my thoughts, and I said I know I'm not drunk, but I thought the little wine I did have was playing tricks on me. Harry is supposed to be in Detroit. I slowly walk over to him, and I pat him, like, 'Are you for real?' He is looking at me like I have lost my mind, and I also think he was truly surprised to find me there. He said, "Cora Shannon," and he hugged me. I died and went to heaven in that moment. The world stood still, and he and I had just gotten off.

When I caught my breath and was able to talk like someone with some sense, he introduced me to his friend, who would later become my brother-in-law. I said, 'Hi,' and went right back to Harry. I learned he was attending San Jose State. Of course, phone numbers were exchanged, and at that time, I heard someone calling my name. It was Jake who wanted to go. I left Harry, and Jake said, "Who or what did you see?" You look different and are acting differently. I said, 'I saw a long-lost friend.' That seemed to suffice for a minute, but when we got to his apartment, which was out of this world with a bear rug in front of the fireplace and a view out of this world, my mind was not there. Instead of us making love, we talked for hours. He was adjusting to his accomplishments and what he was going to do from there. Although we would have made a great couple because we were really into each other, and he was my type, not only because of his looks, but also because of his values and manners. But my true love was in the back of my mind, and I couldn't wait to get home to call him. Jake took me home after a nightcap and a very long kiss. It was as if he knew I wouldn't be coming back.

Reunited with Harry

The next day, Harry called me. We were still trying to catch up from when he left me in Memphis. He said he wanted to come up and see me. He came up the next week with his friend. We continued to talk, and he told me he had been selected to represent the U.S. in the Olympics in Rome. I pretended to be excited for him, but I know you won't believe this. I didn't know anything about the Olympics and how significant this was. He was on the team with Muhammad Ali (whose name was Cassius Clay at that time), and his coach was Mendez from San Jose State. He asked his friend to look after me while he was gone, and his friend came up later to look after me, but not in the way Harry was talking about. I think this became a sore spot with him, and when he later married my best friend Pat, he told her he didn't want her to be my friend.

Harry returned from the Olympics, but not before sending me a postcard saying how tough the competition was in the ring and the women. You know I got furious with him. I turned his friend down, and here he is writing me about other women. That was Harry. I seemed to be his girlfriend, confidant, and sometimes mother. He worked for Mr. Young. He had a patrol business, and Harry worked the dispatch. He also would call me, and we would talk, go to sleep, and wake up talking. Mr. Young said he was running up his bill and wanted to know who was important that he talked to for that long and about what. Mr. Young loved Harry, and he would tease him, but he never really cared about the calls.

My Journey Through Life, Love, and Tragedy

Harry was being pressured for money by his mother. Harry was the oldest of four boys. Two were by her first husband in Memphis, and two were for her husband in Detroit. Harry was always the responsible one. He took care of his brother from Memphis. His brother did nothing but drink and womanize. He was considered the most handsome of the two because of his blond curly hair and fair skin. Harry was the most handsome one to me. He turned pro in order to get money for his mom and help take care of his brother. Mr. Young was his manager, and when he had his first pro fight in San Jose, my girlfriend Minnie and I went to the fight. It was so funny, we looked like the Bobsy twins. We wore black sheath dresses with a red overlay and two large black buttons on the red overlay. Harry had arranged our seating, and when we walked into that arena, I must say we did turn heads. After the fight, Harry had one of his friends bring us to the after party, and somehow, Minnie went with a man at the party, and I went with Harry. We were to meet the next day and come home. We spent the night together, and the next morning, there was a knock on the door. He told me to answer it and to put on his new house slippers. There stood a blond woman, and she was shocked to see me, but I later learned she was angry because I was wearing the slippers she had given him. She asked if he was home, and I said to come in. I went into the bedroom to tell him, and he said he didn't want to talk to her. I said I thought he should. I don't know why I said that. Anyway, he put on his pants and went into the living room, and I shut the door. All I could make out was that she was upset, and so was he. I later learned that she was his girlfriend until he found out she was cheating on him. That's why he sent me to answer the door wearing her slippers. She finally left, and we made love again and then got dressed to meet Minnie. I didn't want to leave him. I always felt he would go away again, and I wouldn't see him again. Little did I know. Harry continued to fight, and he would find me at every fight, nodding to let me know he saw me.

Seeing about Mama

My mother suffered a stroke. She was on her way to babysit and had a stroke. I always get choked up knowing she was in the street and had the stroke, and why. Each of us girls took turns going down to help. I was the last one to go. When I was there, I met the guy I mentioned at the beginning of the book. The pastor was so happy I was there. I hadn't seen him since our conversation in San Francisco. He offered to take me to and from the hospital every day. I was grateful for that because again, my parents didn't have a car. My mother worked very hard to get her strength back. My mother had a lot of pride, and she was determined to walk without a cane. Her doctor had been her doctor for as long as I could remember, and she adored him. He was light, bright, and damn near white and married to one of the biggest family daughters of one of the largest denominations in the U.S.. He was also a player. He and the nurses would stand at the door every morning I came in to see what I had on. As I said, I bought clothes, clothes, and more clothes. I had on a pair of black pumps that I wore with everything. They had special heels and were handmade by the famous shoe designer, Margaret Jerrold. They were very expensive and very beautiful shoes.

My mom's doctor was also the head of the Methodist Hospital. He started off flirting with me by asking silly questions. After three weeks, he finally asked me out. I told my aunt, and she was ecstatic, but my uncle was there, and he said, "You don't have to do anything you don't want to do." I know you think harshly of me for this, but my father didn't have the money to pay for the time my mother was in there. They didn't have health insurance at that time. He had a running bill at the pharmacy for her medicine. I felt that we could negotiate her bill. I thought we were going out to a nice place when I realized he was well-known, and his wife was well-known all over Memphis. So, we went to his office, and in the upper part, there were complete living quarters. I was a little disappointed. My mother was released the next week from the hospital, and all that was in arrears were her life insurance policies. I called all my brothers and asked if they could send money to bring her life insurance up to date. I got no commitment. I think LaRaine paid it.

Navigating Family and Friendships
Mr. Young was taking care of my bills for me. He called me one day and said I really needed to come back. Harry had suffered his first defeat and was beaten pretty badly. They ran a scan on his brain, but didn't see anything. They both said it was because I wasn't there. That made me feel wanted, but I was worried. I did not and do not like fighting of any kind.

After getting Mama home, I really didn't want to leave her, but I had to keep my job. My mother looked at me so sadly that I wanted to cry. She did say to me that her boys had always been her favorites, and I tell you why when I write her story, but her girls had been there for her, and she had it wrong all those years. I was glad she acknowledged it, but it couldn't and wouldn't fill the void of the love I sought from her. I loved and still love my mama, but I never did feel like she loved me as much as I loved her.

The Hardest Fight of My Life
I flew home the week of Easter. When Harry and I got together, my son, Harry, was conceived. He was scheduled for a rematch on May 15, 1961. I told Mr. Young I was pregnant. He asked, "Are you sure?"

I told him, "Yes."

"Promise me you won't tell Harry. It could interfere with his concentration on the fight," he pleaded.

I told Harry, and I am so happy to this day that I followed my mind. "What do you want to do?" he asked me.

"I want to get married," I replied.

He said, "We will get married after the fight because this is my last fight."

I don't like professional boxing. After he told Mr. Young, he said he would try to get Harry a job with the San Francisco Athletic Commission. He said that because he couldn't support a family through boxing. Mr. Young had purchased a 1961 convertible Cadillac, and he was going to let us use it to go to Reno. We really couldn't decide if we wanted Reno or Tahoe. It didn't matter to me. Harry called me before the fight and told me where my seat was, and "Don't you be jumping up, hurting my son."

I laughed. "How do you know you're having a son?"

"I was told that," he responded.

I never knew who or what told him. I thought I would ask him on the way to our wedding. My friend Carl and his girlfriend were going with us to be witnesses. A lot of my friends from the phone company came. I don't know if it was to see us off or what, because they never came to his fights.

We got to the stadium and found our seats, and as always, Harry gave me a nod of acknowledgement. I don't remember the round when he slipped and fell. He was not the same after that. They kept asking him if he was alright, and I think it's instinct that boxers say yes. After the fight, he went to his corner and fell over. They rushed him to the Park

Does God Have Favorites?

Emergency next to Kezar Stadium and determined that he was hemorrhaging from the brain. They rushed him to St. Luke, and before we could get there, they had him in the operating room. I was not his wife officially, so I couldn't sign anything. I called Harry's brother, Marvin, and told him to get there as soon as he could. He came, he must have taken a rocket from San Jose because it seemed one minute I was on the phone with him and the next he was coming in the door. Mr. Young already told us he had to go to Hawaii for an important meeting. He called and told me not to leave the hospital.

"What if he is in the hospital more days than I have off?" I asked.

He said, "Don't worry about it, I will take care of you. Have my brother, Buster, set you up in the nearest hotel and use my credit card."

I told him I would stay with Harry no matter what. Carl stayed with me. He was a Godsend at that time, and later he became distant. I don't know why, but as the saying goes, people come into your life for a reason, a season, or forever. We were high school buddies, and like Pappy, Nick's nickname for Kendall, he was part of my life. Anyway, they brought Harry from the ER and put him in a room. He had a tube in every opening of his body, it seemed. It didn't seem real that only a short while ago, he was smiling and whole. When they got him settled, I went in to talk to him. Of course, he was in a coma and still sedated, but I felt he could hear me. When I touched him, he would flinch; they say those were his reflexes.

I went to the chapel and prayed and prayed for God to let Harry live. I tried to make deals with God, only to find out later that you can't. I was in the twilight zone. I wanted to wake up and be alright. All of our plans were in shambles. We called his mother, and Mr. Young sent her a ticket. She was to arrive the next night at 9:30 pm. I stayed all night thinking, waiting, watching, and praying.

The next morning, Carl suggested that he take me home to change out of my clothes. I still had on my little white wedding dress. He had to assure me Harry would be alright if I left the hospital. You can tell what state of mind I was in to think Carl or anyone else knew that information. But I believed him, and he took me home. I changed into a pair of pants and, of course, Harry's sweater. We immediately went back to the hospital. I did feel more comfortable. I immediately went into his room, and there was no change. I don't know how Aunt Clara found out, but she and some of my telephone friends came over to sit with me. She brought me a pretty white bible that she took back later. We all went and prayed, and they left. Right after they left, they began to take buckets of ice into the room and pack him in ice. I later found out he had begun to bleed again. I became upset and started to cry. I didn't know what was wrong; I just felt he had turned for the worse, although I still held out hope. Buster, Mr. Young's brother, said to come and ride with him to the airport to see Harry's mother come in. I didn't want to, but he insisted, and I was so tired at this point that I didn't have the energy to argue. I rode with him, but I didn't get out. I wanted to get back to the hospital. Marvin had gone earlier and was already there to greet his mother. Buster came back and said her plane was delayed until 11:30 pm. On the way back, Buster said they had announced on the radio that Harry Campbell had died at 9:30 pm. I never heard it because when it started, Buster turned the radio off. He didn't want me to hear it that way. Marvin had gotten to the hospital before us, and when we came in, they were trying to subdue him. He was running the hall, butting his head against the wall. We were told Harry died at 9:30 pm, which was the same time his mother's flight was to land. I was blank in mind and body. I kept saying, "When is this dream going to end. I have to wake up, I have to wake up."

    I remember Buster holding on to the counter. I remember Carl saying gently, "Cora, let me take you home." He said I looked at him, but I was not there. He took me by the arm and led me outside. I saw all the cars passing by and I said to him, "Where is everybody going." Poor Carl, he didn't know what to say. I said, "Don't they know Harry's dead?"

    I wanted everything to stop because I thought if it stopped, I would wake up out of this dream. Carl finally got me home, and I went into that apartment. When I was alone, I cried myself to sleep. Harry's mother and brother came to the apartment. She wanted to stay there. I told her I only had a mattress on the floor and two floor pillows in the living room. She became upset with me because I didn't want her to stay, and there really was no place for her to stay. I guess that turned the tide with her against me. I needed and wanted to be alone. Somehow, when I experience trouble or death, I want to be alone, and most people think you shouldn't and want to keep you company. I need to seek God or whatever I need alone in the quiet of my space.

    Mr. Young called me two days later and asked if I could meet him in San Francisco. When a wrestler or boxer turns pro, they are automatically in a fund that is given to the most needy members of their family. They were having this hearing to see who was going to receive the money. Of course, Mr. Young had tried everything to get it for me, but again, we didn't have the papers. He even suggested that we go to Mexico and get a marriage certificate. I told him his mother would contest that because she knew we weren't married. He then said I'll take you to Mexico to get an abortion. "It's going to be hard on you, honey, trying to raise him by yourself," he said.

"Under no circumstances will I do anything to hurt or get rid of this baby. This is all that is left of Harry. I am going to have this baby," I insisted.

"I will support you any way I can," he promised. And believe me, he did.

After the commission told him there was no way I could receive the money, maybe his mother would consider giving me some for the child. Mr. Young brought me up there in hopes she would consider giving me some of the money. He spoke with her before they called her in for an interview and asked her to consider setting aside some money for the child. If she promised, he would plead for them to give her the maximum. She told Mr. Young, "She should have thought of that before she got pregnant." That incensed Mr. Young, and he went back in, and I don't know what he told them, but she and his brother got plane tickets to take the body to Memphis and to return to their respective homes. That was it. She had a funeral for Harry, and if his brother hadn't told me, I would have never known. She didn't want me to sit in the front row. His brother told me to come and sit next to him. His brother was wearing Harry's suit, which he was going to wear to our wedding, and they had bought Harry a top from the morgue. You could see where they had cut and opened up his head. I wanted to scream. I couldn't wait to get out of there. That wasn't Harry, and I don't know why she did that. She should have flown him home to be buried in the National Cemetery in Memphis and not have an open casket.

Harry was a paratrooper. I found out later that she went to the Social Security office to see if she could get his Social Security. They asked her if there were any children or if there were going to be any children. She said under oath that there were none. Of course, there was no DNA at that time.

Part 7

Struggling with Grief, Motherhood, Marriage & Betrayal

Chapter 13: One Heartbreak After Another

I was still working at the phone company, and when I went back to work, as I said, they started in on me for whatever reason. Before I went back, Aunt Clara came over and literally packed my things and brought me to her house. I felt awkward going there after all that they had done to me. I wanted to think she had come to realize I had never and would never have any interest in her husband. She saw her opportunity to have a baby, and she did everything to make me comfortable. She took advantage of my vulnerability. I was in an unexplainable state. A scene came into my mind that helped me also move back. I once went with Pat and my brother-in-law to a house in San Francisco. He was there to see a friend. The men were in the back room playing cards, and there was a young lady in the front room with her baby asleep on a dirty sofa. I said to myself I would never do that if I had a baby. I wouldn't let him or her sleep on someone's nasty sofa. I would not pull them around with me. I wanted a stable environment for them. But it was always something I couldn't explain about my feelings for Aunt Clara. Although I respected her as I was raised to do, I never really had the feeling I had when I was a little girl and when I first came to California.

Aunt Clara's Intervention

When I went back to work, they gave me fits. They said I wasn't working up. They said I was spending all my money on clothes, and I wouldn't have any money for the baby. The supervisor would listen in on me and call me out for the tiniest of infractions. I came home crying one day, and Aunt Clara asked what was wrong, and I told her how they were treating me at the phone company. She called the next day and got the Chief Operator on the phone. She said, "Cora has been coming home crying and in a depressed state because of the harassment she is receiving from the phone company."

"This is highly irregular for a family member to call on behalf of an employee," the Chief Operator stated.

"With what Cora has been through and is going through, she does not need any more undue pressure from you. If she loses this baby or some harm comes to it because of her state of mind that is affecting her body, we will own the phone company. I want to assure you, whether she works there or not, she will not be on welfare. None of my family has been on welfare, so you can stop pressuring her. She has been through and is going through enough." Aunt Clara threatened.

The next day, the atmosphere was completely different. "What did you need for the baby? We want to give you a baby shower, if that's alright."

"I have everything I need." And I did. "Thanks, but no thanks."

Harry's Birth and the Early Days
It came time for me to take maternity leave. Harry weighed 10 pounds even and was 21 inches long. He was a beautiful baby. He was born Jan. 6, 1962, and his dad was born on Jan. 7th. Mr. Young had set up a little fund for him from some of the fellow boxers and newspaper people. His birth was announced in the San Francisco Chronicle. Aunt Clara finally had a baby. When I came out of the hospital and went to reach for the baby, she was in the back seat with him. Mr. Young bought him this set that cost $300, but it could be converted into a carriage, a high chair, a stroller, and then a table and chair. He had everything. I got him sterling silver diaper pins with his name and birthdate. I went back to the phone company, and one of my friends from high school had her baby a week before Harry, and she said she would babysit him. Aunt Clara did not like it because every time she came to get him, he was wet and crying. Her baby was dry and happy. We found another lady to keep him, and she was very good. Things began to get back into a rhythm; the only thing that bothered me was when Harry was older and could talk. I worked broken shifts, and he would cry for me not to leave him when I would go home between shifts. I would go back to work in a horrible state. I stopped coming home between shifts. When Christmas came, I thought I would get it off because it was my time to get it off, but they said my Christmas was

when I was on maternity leave. I asked, "How could that be when I'm not in the count for the office?"

I had to work. Before I went back to work, Pat came to see the baby. She brought these handsome guys with her. I told her not to come because I looked terrible. I gained 79 pounds with Harry, and my hair was not done, but she came anyway. I'll never forget it because it snowed that year in San Francisco. She showed up with this handsome man in ivory pants and a blue double-breasted coat. He was very nice, and Aunt Clara was trying to get me into this dress, and I finally had to wear my robe. Hair all over my head. I whispered to her that I was going to get her for that. She laughed and said I gotcha. He knew what to say. He invited me to a party that he said he was giving in six weeks. He knew that's when you are considered to resume your activities. Sure enough, in six weeks, Pat and I went to this party.

This house, where he and six others lived, was near San Francisco State. Harry's friend, my future brother-in-law, his brother Albert, whom I ended up marrying, and others whose names I can't use were there. It was a nice party, but I stayed in the living room because they had a nice fire going, and I became nostalgic. He soon came and began to talk and give me some attention. We became an item even when they moved to the Haight. He was a player and had a game. All the women liked him; he was so cute.

My friend Pat went with his brother. His brother worked, but my friend did not; he said he was an air traffic controller and he was waiting to get assigned to Monterey Airport. We, not thinking at that time, should have known he was a con artist. We went over there nearly every weekend. I thought I was in love again. He asked me to marry him and gave me a ring. The diamond was so small you needed a magnifying glass to see it, but when you are in love, who cares? My friends at the phone company were happy for me, and they were planning wedding showers. Christmas came, and he didn't show up or call. New Year's came, and he came the day after with all kinds of excuses. In the meantime, the jeweler called me to see if I had the ring and asked if I would return it because he hadn't paid for it. I told the jeweler I would return it to the person who had bought it. I told him when he came about the jeweler's call, and he could have his ring and not to bother with an explanation. I told him I had one male to take care of, and it didn't include him.

I was more disappointed than hurt. I was still wounded from Harry's death, and this person lulled me into some comfort. He was handsome and knew what to say to make you feel good about yourself and him. We shared some very tender moments. But I didn't realize how fragile I still was.

My friend broke up with his brother also, and the next thing I knew was that she was marrying the man who would become my future brother-in-law, and my ex was paralyzed by a woman's husband who shot him. I felt bad about that, but you have to be careful who you fool with. Eventually, the whole household split apart, and everyone went their separate ways. I can say we had some really good times there.

My Return to Faith

I begin to get weary and worn. With Harry asking where his daddy was and clinging to my leg to stop me from going back to work, I was at my wits' end. Every time he asked where his daddy was, I would want to scream. A knife would pierce my heart. I had such righteous indignation against God. *Why did Harry have to die, and all these no-good bums walking the streets? How can you say you love me and take away my love?*

I decided to go and try to find that place. I walked into the Catholic church. It was peaceful and quiet, and I began to try to commune with God, to try and get some answers. A priest came up to me out of nowhere and said, "I understand you want to talk to me." I was totally perplexed. I had not asked to talk with him, but after I thought about it, this was my answer to asking God for help. I went to the rectory, and we talked for hours. He was a wonderful Priest. He would come to my apartment, sit on the floor, drink wine, and talk. We talked and talked. I didn't always understand or agree with what he was saying, but the door was beginning to open to bring me back to my faith. After three years, I finally became Catholic. It took that long because I would not agree to some concepts. The pastor relented. I would be baptized, and he would just pray. Harry was also christened Catholic.

Tears for Mama

I came home one day, and Aunt Clara was acting kind of funny. She didn't know how to tell me, but she came up to me and said, "Your mom died today." It was December 13, 1965. I will never forget that date. I had said I was going home that summer before, but I put it off. I took

My Journey Through Life, Love, and Tragedy

Harry home when he was 16 months old. We got a chance to see his paternal grandfather and aunts. They adored him, and I feel bad that I didn't take him back to see them the next day as I had promised. His grandfather would not take a picture of him and insisted we come back the next day, and he and all of them would take a picture. I knew in my mind I would not come back because it was so difficult to get to their house. They were disappointed, and later, I was too, because we still have no pictures of them.

We had to decide how we were going home. My brother and his family didn't have the money to fly, and neither did I. It was also too dangerous to drive between California and Memphis at that time of year due to the weather. My Aunt Margaret in Chicago offered to help anyone needing money to go. I asked Aunt Clara if she would ask for me, and I would pay her back when I returned. She said she would. When I told the phone company that my mother had passed, they immediately sent one of the operators to San Francisco to get my check, and the office raised $125.00 in collections for me. I was so thankful to them that they thought enough of me to give that amount in such a short time. When I went to pick up my check, they gave me the money they had raised. Stupid me went home and told Aunt Clara what they had done. She had gotten the money from Aunt Margaret, the amount I never knew, because she asked me, now that I had money, how much of the money I wanted that Aunt Margaret had sent? I told her that I wanted it all because I thought it had been asked for in my name. She said she was not giving me all of the money. I told her that if they needed extra money for Mama's burial, I wanted to contribute. She said the boys should be responsible for that. We decided to take the bus. It was the cheapest way for all of us to travel. It was also a trip from hell and back. It was long, and the rest stops were nasty and unsanitary. We went into one of the places to eat, and my brother ordered grits that came with rat droppings in them. I didn't eat or drink hardly anything except the lunch we had packed. It took us three days to get to Memphis. I was completely worn out. I promised myself I would never take a bus again anywhere that wasn't local or to Reno.

I stayed with my niece Elizabeth because I usually stayed at her house when I visited Memphis. The family's house was full. People brought tin tubs of chicken, the bakery sent every type of pastry imaginable, and the outpouring of sympathy was overwhelming. My oldest brother came home, and I couldn't wait to see him. I went up to him and he asked, "Who are you?" I said, "I'm your baby sister." He grabbed me and held me for a long time. That felt like a void had finally been filled in my life. My brothers and sisters had a meeting in Mama's bedroom. My oldest brother and I were not included. I didn't know why they were meeting without us until my brother came out and said he was looking for his checkbook. I asked him why. He said that Mama had always wanted to be put into a vault, and they were going to put money together to get her one. I said, "Why wasn't I included?"

He said, "If you feel that way, you can pay my share."

I was so hurt. First, my mother is dead; secondly, Aunt Clara wouldn't give me the money that was borrowed in my name, and thirdly, they had excluded me from a decision about my mother. It was as if Tony and I were not a part of the family. I began to fuss and tell Aunt Clara about not giving me the money that I could have contributed. My oldest sister came out and told me I better not say anything to Aunt Clara about that money. I felt so betrayed and alone. Aunt Clara's feelings were more important than mine. I cry every time I think of this, and I'm crying as I write this. I guess it is really true about your birth order. Mine was completely forgotten. I felt like a non-entity or person. I don't think or know how they hurt me by not including me or respecting me as a member of the family. People always say that I am spoiled because I'm the baby of the family. I was never spoiled. I feel my brothers and sisters really didn't consider me as part of them. I think that's why family means so much to me. I always wanted to be a part of a large group. I think because of their actions, I formed my actions and thoughts about family. I never wanted any of my children or grandchildren to suffer the pains I endured. I realize in some ways that it was not fair to them to take away some of the consequences they should have had to endure. You can take away some of the things you don't want them to endure, but they should suffer some responsibilities for their actions. I realize now it's the only way they learn to grow and cope.

The next day was Saturday, and we had my mom's wake. It didn't seem my mother was dead until I saw her in the casket. When I went up to the casket to see her, she looked beautiful. My oldest sister had done her hair in what we used to call a marcel and had made herself up to look very natural. I saw the burn marks on the back of her hands, and I began to fall. The pastor came to help, and my sister told him she would take care of me. I think by this time, they had found out he had a relationship with me.

My Journey Through Life, Love, and Tragedy

    The next day was Sunday. They scheduled her funeral service during Sunday worship. This was highly unusual. They left her body in the church from Saturday to the next day of the funeral. The pastor said he knew she was happy that she had spent the night in the church. She loved the church. She found solace and peace in serving in many different capacities. It was her life. The next day, we all gathered at my mama's house to ride to the funeral. LaRaine, my oldest sister, told all the boys that they would not cry over her mother today. She said that she had done all the crying, and they had not done or acted the way they should toward their mother. She said, "When I called and wrote to you to send her a little money, you didn't respond or had to ask your wives. So, you will not cry today, or I will mop up Trinity Church with you."
    They all knew LaRaine would do what she said. Then my oldest brother, Tony, said, 'And nobody better be drunk."
    That broke the awkward moment, and everybody laughed because he would be the only one drunk. I don't remember most of the service. I was completely in my own world of sorrow. My niece and I sat side by side, and it looked like we were trying to outdo each other, crying. My mother babysat her like she did her brother. She said every day they would kneel at the sink to pray. We were all in our memories. When we got out of church, I got into the limousine. I wanted to be alone, and most of my brothers and sisters were surrounded by the people they knew.
    One man came up and asked if I wasn't going to speak to him. I said, "Who are you?"
    He said, "LaRaine, you don't remember me?"
    "I'm not LaRaine," I informed him.
    To which he replied, "Oh, you are the baby girl."
    I said, "Yes. And LaRaine is in back of me."
    He went, and I assumed he found LaRaine. It was such a reunion with them. I remember them telling me that our house was the neighborhood house. They all came to our house. One of the people who came became one of Martin Luther King Jr.'s photographers. He told me I had the sweetest mother. He said she would tell all of them it was time for dinner and they should go home. He said they wouldn't go because they knew if they waited long enough, she would tell them all to come in and eat. These were some of the memories that they were remembering. I was not in that era. LaRaine would often say to me, "Oh shut up, you don't

know what you are talking about, you weren't even born. You were somewhere in Papa's balls."

So, I waited until the others got into the car to ride to the cemetery. We had two police escorts, and it wasn't enough. I have never seen that many cars going to a cemetery before. When they put her in the ground, I begin to shake. Marion looked at me and came and put her arms around me. I said she is going to be cold, and I couldn't stop shaking. Even though my mom and I had our disagreements, I loved her and still do love her. When we left the cemetery, there were cars still trying to get into the cemetery. I don't know why, when a person dies, they become Saints. My mother was often vilified and talked about taking over and trying to boss everything. Now she had all of these people coming to show their respect. Sometimes I feel some people are truly hypocrites. The older I get, the more I appreciate the values, social grace, and love of God and His Son Jesus Christ that she instilled in me. She was truly a remarkable person, and I still to this day miss her. My wish is that I will see her again.

We left the next day, coming home. The closer we got to the west, the better the scenery and environment became. I was ready to leave Memphis. It only held mixed memories for me. I was happy to get home and see my baby. I missed him. He was always someone to share my love, and he always loved me back. I went back to work, and things began to settle into my regular routine.

Chapter 14: Facing Deception & Heartbreak

 Out of nothing better to do, I went by the house of the man I met in Memphis when my mother was sick. His name was Jesse Mason. He did what he said he was going to do and got to California. He tried to get me to marry him before the baby was born, and I said no. I introduced him to all of my friends, hoping he would like one of them and leave me alone. None of it seemed to work out. Harry was three years old, and for some reason, I decided to stop by his apartment and talk. One thing led to another, and after being asked to marry him a hundred times as a fluke, I said yes. I don't know what came over me. I think I was still going through the motions and not really wanting to be in the real world. We called my niece and told her we were getting married. Once I got over myself, I began to get into it.

 We decided to get married in March, but the Catholic Church does not have celebrations during Lent. I know God was looking out for me because he knew how this was going to turn out. We bought a car that I had to co-sign for because he hadn't been on his job long enough. My girlfriend from Memphis, the majorette, had moved to California and gotten married to one of the Alpha men I used to run around with. They had four boys. Her sister had a bad experience at Tennessee State, and her mother had sent her here to get away from the environment. She called me and asked if I would take her with me when I went out because she was married and couldn't party the way a single person could. I said, "Sure." She began to go with me and my future husband. She would even spend the night sometimes and wear my clothes. I thought we were having fun. I took her with me down to Mr. Young's. He wanted to introduce me to the president of Lockheed. We decided to get married at my aunt's house by her minister. I wore my cotillion dress, and Jesse and I got married with some of my friends as attendants. We really didn't have a reception, but some snacks. I was happy and unhappy. Have you ever had an experience where you knew something was amiss, but you couldn't put your finger on it, as the old folks used to say? Aunt Clara said she would keep Harry until we got settled.

The first thing that upset me was that he was smoking weed and taking all my little extra money to buy it. Secondly, he wouldn't show up to pick me up knowing I didn't have any money for the bus. He would lie and say I didn't come down when you could look out of the window and see the line of cars waiting for us. Of course, I owed Minnie for bus fare. Things were not going well. I asked when we were going to bring Harry over because it had been three months. He had the nerve to ask me why I didn't give him to Aunt Clara? We could have our own children. I reminded him of what he said before we were married. He then dared to say that I had to choose between him and my son. I said "Okay," out of the blue.

The hurts and disappointments were coming so frequently now that I think I was becoming numb. The next day, I didn't go to work.

"You going to work?" he asked, checking to see if I planned to be home, I suppose.

"I'm not feeling well," I answered. When he left for work, I called my brother, and he came with his truck, and we loaded all my things and the things my friends gave me for wedding gifts. My brother took them to his basement, and I went home to my baby. I went back to the apartment the next evening, and when I opened the door, the chain was on it. I looked and saw this red-haired person run into the bathroom.

"Will you come and take the chain off this door so I can come in and get what I came for?" I said.

"Can you come back later? Or I can bring it to you," he suggested. "NO!" I said as I looked through the chained door, seeing clearly who he was with.

"I'm not gonna let you in, 'cause you might hurt her," he said with fear oozing from his voice.

I first couldn't believe my eyes, and now I couldn't believe my ears. First, he is having sex with this person I befriended, and now he is protecting her from me. I was shaking with anger. All of the lying about me not coming down from the office, and his leaving after we got home from work under some flimsy excuse, came to light. They had started this before we got married. Why didn't he have the decency not to get married? Why did she use me and then screw my husband before we got married, and afterwards?

I left and went to my friend's house.

"May I make a collect call?" I asked.

She said, "Of course."

I called the mother of this thing, as I now saw her. Her mother was very perplexed, and she was telling someone in the house that I was calling her collect from California. She finally accepted the call. I told her about her daughter and my husband.

"I just came from my apartment to get an item I had left, and your daughter ran out of the bedroom into the bathroom. I may have become her friend and trusted her, but if she stays here, I can't guarantee her safety," I ranted.

I was hurt enough to really hurt her. Her mother sent for her the next day. I didn't hear from her sister until a year later. I don't know if she was embarrassed or didn't know what to say. I didn't blame her, but I was beginning to think this person and her family have cost me more than anyone should have to bear. She cost me my dream, and her sister cost me my husband.

A month after this happened, the husband saw me coming home from work and pleaded with me to just come and talk to him. I told him that we had nothing to say to each other. He said we are still married. We need to talk. I finally relented and got into the car. He took me up in the hills of Richmond. I was unfamiliar with that area. I suppose he knew because his uncle had once been the mayor of Richmond. He started off by saying he was sorry, and he wanted me to come back and bring the baby. I told him under no circumstances would I ever come back, and we needed to work out the arrangement for the car. If he was going to make the payments, he could have it. He began to cry and told me he was not going to let me go until I promised to come back. At this point, I knew I had to appease him to get home again. I told him I would come back tomorrow if he took me home. He said no, I had to come back today. I said I would if he would take me home to get some clothes. He finally agreed, and I breathed a sigh of relief. He brought me home and waited out front. I ran into the house and told my aunt what had happened, and we should call the police to make him leave. My uncle took his gun and went out and put it to his face and told him to leave and not ever try to contact me again. He would be hearing from my lawyer. I didn't know that at the time; I just saw him leave and told my aunt she didn't have to call the police.

I begin to really question God now. I had fought my way back from the depths, and now it's happening again. This time it's trust and deception. This time I'm again trying to help a friend, and it was a friend I thought of her sister, who was bitten. *When would I learn that it is Scorpion's nature? When would I stop trying to find happiness? When was happiness going to find me? Was I not deserving, had I been a horrible person in another life? Was I still being punished for disobeying my mother? Was I being punished for having a relationship with the pastor and a married man? What was I supposed to do? Where was I supposed to go?* I thought about becoming a Nun. I wouldn't have to worry about anything worldly. But then I had my baby.

It was said that when you have troubles in your life, God is trying to teach you a lesson. I guess I was too dumb to understand what the lessons were and what I was supposed to do about them. I was always told I had a hard head, and I was beginning to believe it.

One day, my Chief Operator had them bring me to her desk. She was on the board of the credit union, and they had sent an order to garnish my wages for the car. It seems that he had not paid for it as promised. She said she wanted to work out a deal so I would only have to pay half, and they would go after him for the other. She worked out a payment plan through payroll, and I eventually paid my half. I don't know if he ever paid his half or not. I didn't see him anymore after that. I learned he married a young lady who sang in a popular gospel group, and they had a son. I also heard he did her wrong, too, and she passed away. At the funeral, he tried to take her out of the casket. I don't know what happened to his son, and the next thing I heard about him, he had moved back to Arkansas and married a doctor. The last time I heard of him was over 10 years ago, and he was said to look very well and happy. I really didn't feel anything about it one way or the other. After going through all the wrongs, I try to forget these people.

A Mother's Determination

I moved on, and I finally got a car. A friend that Minnie had helped get a car wanted someone to take over the payments. It was a Triumph

My Journey Through Life, Love, and Tragedy

TR3 sports car. I was in heaven—no more buses and dealing with people on the streets. One morning, I was waiting at the bus stop, and three men in a convertible, who were drunk, said, "Hey, pretty baby, you sure look good." One of them said, "You ain't gon speak? You ugly we just told that to make you feel good but you ugly." I wanted to dig a hole in the pavement, and the people at the bus stop laughed and laughed.

Now I had a car, and I would pick up Harry, and we would fly down the highway. He would say, "Go fasta Mama." The car was blue, and I bought him a blue outfit to wear while riding in the car. With Harry, I was always stopped by an admiring person. I dressed him like I always wanted to be dressed. He was in a daycare run by a very wonderful Christian Woman. We called her Mama Mills. Many of my friends also took their children to this day care. She would always say she admired us because we dressed our children the same way we dressed ourselves.

Life fell into a routine. My friends and I at the phone company would party. We would all be so sleepy that we wished the customers would go away. The funny thing about it is that we would all resolve to go home and sleep until someone said that someone was having a get-together, and we would forget all about sleep. I moved in with a friend whose mother worked at the barber shop as a manicurist.

This was a time before I had a car, and my aunt would get into these moods, asking and doing things that were out of the clear blue sky. I was getting ready to go somewhere, and all of a sudden, my aunt asked, "Who's going to keep Harry?"

When things like this happened, I'd want to keep myself at home. It was shades of Memphis. All of a sudden, she was trying to start controlling me again. This woman, who wouldn't let me fix his formula because she said I didn't wash my hands, who would go to the laundromat and run the machines with hot water so Harry's clothes wouldn't touch anyone else's dirt, this person who took my child everywhere she went except work, now wanted to know who was going to keep Harry.

I told her, "I thought you were going to keep him like you always have."

She said, "I can't keep him all the time."

"What?!" I said, half confused and half angry. "Okay, you don't have to keep him at all. I will get him tomorrow".

I came and got Harry, and we went to the apartment. I had to get up and take him on the bus to daycare and then take another bus to work.

Does God Have Favorites?

Needless to say, I was late, and the telephone company really frowned on tardiness, but I wasn't going to let her or anyone else tell me what to do, question my behavior, or try to run my life.

Of course, that evening when I got home from work, there was a knock at the door. She sends the uncle to ask if I would let Harry come home. She was too chicken to come herself. I really didn't or couldn't understand her. I later found out why she said and did things for and to me. I let him go because the buses alone were too much for me to handle. But that never happened again. I could say I was going to the ends of the earth, and she would say, 'Okay, be careful.'

I'm never getting married again.
Marie and her family had moved back to California. She was married with two beautiful girls. We began to take the children to all kinds of places. We took them to Fairyland, and a place near Santa Cruz that I can't recall, but we drove hours to get there. We took them to the State Fair in Sacramento. We took them to the aquarium, museums —you name it —we took them. One day, I visited her house, and the brother of one of our classmates was also there. He looked just like his sister. Of course, a conversation occurred, and we began seeing each other. He was an alcoholic, and I didn't know it until later. I'm like my mother in that we both were turned off by people who drank and got drunk. When we went out, he was fun to be with. He would drink but didn't get drunk. One day, I came home, and he had bought food and stocked my refrigerator. The next thing I knew, he was staying more and more. He had a little boy, and he was really cute. He would bring him over, and we would play with him, but I had a child, and I really didn't want another one, especially one that belonged to another woman. Somehow, one thing led to another, and he asked me to marry him. You would think a bell would have gone off in my head, but it didn't. I sometimes think, *why did I want to get married again after my last disaster?* I really can't say except that I like the state of marriage. I thought it was two people committing themselves to each other, but there are so many extraneous things that go along with that, and my needs overrode my mind.

We went to Reno and got married. We stopped by Aunt Clara's and told her. We went back to the apartment, and the phone rang. It is the mother of his little boy. After stating who she was, she went on to say, "I need to tell you that the man you just married is still married to me."

I almost fainted.

"I didn't call to cause you any problems. And I don't plan to go and have him declared a bigamist. I just felt you should know."

"Thank you for telling me," I said, as I ended the call and then proceeded to ask him, "Why?!"

He feigned innocence. He thought they were divorced because he signed the papers. I went the next week and filed for an annulment. It wasn't soon enough that he took my car and wrecked it, and I am broke and can't get it fixed. Insurance hadn't become a necessity, so my car is inoperable, and I am a guest at another friend's wedding. I had to seek a ride with another friend, and I was in no mood to attend a reception, but I managed to make it through, and the bride's mother praised me for doing a wonderful job.

Here I go again. I'm really through now with everything. I moved back to Aunt Clara's and began to concentrate on my son. I was so depressed for the hundredth time. I was never going to get married again or have a relationship with a man again. Little did I know that my life was going to take a turn that I would have never dreamed of or thought of.

A Glimpse of Hope

It was 1967. New Year's was two weeks away. A young man in Richmond gave New Year's Eve parties for as long as I could remember. For some reason, I never went, but most of my friends attended, and they would always say, "You need to come, everybody we know is there." Marie called, "Cora, I want you to go with us to this year's New Year's Eve party."

"No, Marie. I am not going," I told her in no uncertain terms. I had had it with life and men. Besides, I have no one to kiss at midnight. That settles it. I am not going."

"You can kiss her husband. I don't care, but this year you're going," she insisted.

New Year's Eve came, and I was watching TV, being a grump. I was all alone, but I wasn't being hurt or disappointed by anybody either. Around 10 o'clock, I hear these heels coming up the steps. It's Marie. "Get up and get dressed," she demanded.

"I told you I was not going!" I resisted.

"Yes, you are," as she went through my closet picking out a dress. She got the dress and said, "Get dressed, I am not leaving until you put this on. We are going to my friend's mother's house for gumbo and then to the party."

I grudgingly got dressed and went. I didn't even care what I had on, but I remember it was a light green knit dress and white at the top. I still wore the same Margaret Jerrold shoes, and I had those on, but I don't remember the coat. Little did I know that attending this New Year's Eve party would change my life forever.

Part 8

New Hope

Chapter 15: Meeting Albert

As I stated before, I was forced to go to this New Year's Eve party not knowing what was in store for me. My sister-in-law had told me that Albert had moved in with them. She said that he and his wife were getting a divorce, and it seemed that she had left, taking all the furniture, leaving him with only a cot and a blanket to sleep on. He decided to move, and he counter-filed for a divorce.

In 1967, there was no such thing as a no-fault divorce. In 1970, you could get a divorce due to irreconcilable differences, which was less punitive because no one was at fault.

Albert was in business with three other people, and they had a big contract and were doing well. My sister-in-law was telling me that Albert was giving her all kinds of money, and she and her other friend were having a ball spending it. She also said she was going to introduce him to her friend. I didn't give any of this a thought. On the night of the party, after we had gone to one of our other friends' houses and had gumbo, we went to the party. I walked in, and there were wall-to-wall people because this was a little house. The host had cleared one room for dancing. Marie and her husband immediately went into the kitchen, where drinks were being served. Before I could follow, I looked up and saw Albert.

Let me tell you how I met Albert, so you'll know how I recognized him. Harry was a good friend of his brother, and one time, I went to San Jose, and I went to his home and met all of his family.

He spoke and asked, "What are you doing these days?"

"Nothing but working." I didn't bother to go into the business of my two marriages because they were over.

"You want to dance?" he asked.

"Yes," and we went into the other room and began dancing.

Dancing Through Uncertainty
After dancing through two songs, we stood and started talking again. I asked him, "Did you come with someone?"

"Yes," he answered. But he didn't disclose her name. After being in his company, I became uncomfortable because he said he had brought someone else, and I didn't or couldn't understand why he was taking so much time with me. I told him I was going to the kitchen to get a drink. "What are you drinking?" he asked. "I'll go and get it for you."

I wanted to go because I wanted to talk with Marie about him not leaving my side. Thank goodness she came into the dance room. I told her, "Look, Marie, I feel uncomfortable because he hasn't left me since we greeted each other."

"Why should you care about his date? Obviously, he wants to be with you. Lighten up," she advised.

I felt a little better because his date could have come and interrupted at any time, but she didn't. I found out from my sister-in-law who he had brought to the party the next day. Her name was Barbara Bridgewater. I was somewhat shocked because she was very well-known and highly respected, having been a child prodigy.

Before leaving, he asked, "Will you go out with me?"

"Where would you like to take me?" I responded.

"Name it."

"I want to go to the Playboy Club," I quickly replied.

"Here's my number. Call me," he said as he handed me his card.

I really wanted to go to the Playboy Club because it was all the rage, and he had a key, but I knew I would never call him. I felt he should have asked for my number and called me if he was interested. I called my sister-in-law the next day.

"Albert's going to take me to the Playboy Club," I told her.

"I'm going too," she said.

"Okay," I said, because I really thought he wouldn't call after me, especially after I did not give him my number. I went along with my usual routine and was planning Harry's birthday party. He called, and I was happy, I don't know why, because I had sworn I would not get involved again, so that I wouldn't get hurt again. I also felt that going out with him was not a commitment but just a date, and I was determined that was all it was going to be.

My Journey Through Life, Love, and Tragedy

We made a date on Harry's birthday, and I thought that was ok because Harry's party would be over long before our date. He and his brother surprised me and came to Harry's birthday party.

I had some white patent leather boots on hold in San Francisco, and after the party, he took Harry and me to San Francisco with some of his balloons tied to the car. Harry had a great time and was extremely excited. Now I'm beginning to get nervous. He went home to get dressed, and I went upstairs to get dressed. I was a wreck, trying to figure out what to wear - the boots or the silver stockings with this purple dress - and dealing with my emotions about him.

I started to call him to ask if we could go another time. I begin to think that you had to have had a reservation, and because the club was new, everybody who belonged wanted to go. If and when you get the reservation, you had better take it, because it might be a long time before getting another. I really wanted to see and say I had been to the Playboy Club. He came to get me, and he really had on a beautiful suit and tie. He complimented me on my looks and we started to the club. Once we got in, he ordered drinks and snacks. We talked, and I took a look around. I went to the restroom, and the bunnies commented and complimented me on my outfit and stockings. I thanked them and felt good that I had chosen the right outfit. Albert bought me a Playboy mug, and we started home.

He said, "You have to pay for parking."

At first, I was angry and felt like, *What is this? He has spent a lot of money in the club, and now he is asking me to pay for parking? That is like asking me to pay him for taking me out.* I paid for the parking, although I didn't have any money left, because I had spent all my money on the party and the boots. I later thought it was ok because now I'm not obligated. I got what I wanted to go to the Playboy Club, and I was satisfied. No strings, no attachment, and I am sticking to my guns. Well, when we got to my house, I was cold, and he put his coat on me. And when he kissed me goodnight, he asked me out again and said he enjoyed my company; the iceberg began to melt. He also didn't ask for his coat back. I didn't think of it until I went inside, and it was too late to give it back. I often wondered if we both had deliberately had me keep the coat, and I deliberately forgot to give it back.

We began to go out steady, and I was starting to have fun. First, he always treated me like a lady; he was not demanding, he was so smart and interesting to talk to, and we went to places I had never gone before. But the most important thing to me was that he kept his word.

Pat asked me to go with her to this meeting of a club called the *Civic Organization for Black Awareness*. I went and thought they had a good premise. By being in clerical positions, I began to take minutes because the secretary was supposedly sick. Albert's brother believed that mentioning Barbara Bridgewater's name would add status to the club. He is and was such a social climber. Then there was no mention of her coming to the meetings. I fell into the routine of a secretary and began working, selling tickets for different fundraisers. I also went to churches to ask for their participation. When they distributed literature with her name listed as the secretary, I began to balk. By the way, this is the same person Albert took to the New Year's Eve party. I suppose her name carried more weight and would garner more attention than mine. I was going to drop out and let them have it, but another young man who was very interested in me tried to talk me out of it and also asked me out. I don't know how Albert got wind of it, but he came down hard on his brother and the other members in my defense and told them they were not going to disrespect me, because when they disrespected me, they disrespected him. I was really impressed, but I had lost the feeling for the club, although I thought the club could have been a great asset to the community. It seemed they ended it with a big party, and my sister-in-law really wanted me to go, but I didn't feel comfortable around them, and also the young man who wanted me to go out with him. I was attracted to him and conflicted about my feelings. I didn't want or need any conflict of interest at this juncture of our relationship. Albert didn't go either, and we went to a Warriors' game.

Albert became more and more important to me. He was such a delight compared to the others; I call garbage the ones I went out with and married. He was a person of his word. He didn't play games, and he was an unselfish lover. He moved back into the apartment that he and his soon-to-be ex-wife shared. He bought himself a bedroom set. I wasn't aware that when he asked me to come and live with him, it was their old apartment. I often asked why the neighbors never talked to me, and the one across from us always rolled her eyes at me. Once, when her husband was at the door, she asked him, "What are you looking at?"

"The finest thing I've ever seen," he said.

She came and saw it was me, and slammed the door so hard, I think she took the hinges off.

Navigating Family Opinions

Everybody was against my moving in with Albert. My aunt said I couldn't come back if I moved in with him. She said, "Why buy the cow when you can get the milk free?" My sister-in-law said she thought it was sad to have slept with everybody and then not end up with a husband. She called the next day and apologized. I told Albert about the discussion, and he dismissed my sister-in-law's statement. However, he said that if I came to live with him, he would provide enough money for me to get an apartment and be able to live there for six months if our relationship didn't work out. I thought about it for a week and realized that I was staying there more than at Aunt Clara's anyway. I decided I wanted to be with him more than just on dates. I also had some furniture stored at a friend's, and if things worked out, I would bring it so we could have some living room furniture.

Things were going well. There always seemed to be something to come along and mess up a good thing. First, Albert and his partners decided to dissolve the business because they were very upset about Albert's ex-wife auditing their books. It also interfered with them getting other contracts. So, when I moved with Albert, he was finishing up the big contract they had left. He worked late into the night.

The phone calls began from his soon-to-be ex, asking if he was there. I guess the neighbor told her I was staying there with him. I would try to be polite and tell her no, and I would tell him she called. That was not enough for her; she called again.

"May I speak to Albert?"

"Whose calling?" I asked.

"His WIFE!" she exclaimed.

"Oh. You mean his ex-wife?" I snapped back.

"I am coming out there and blow your brains out," she threatened.

"You should be careful because they sell guns to more than you. I'm sure you would hate to see me raising your daughter," I countered. That was a red flag.

She said, "I'm on my way."

I called Albert. "Your ex-wife called, and when I let her know I wasn't intimidated by her, she threatened to come and blow my brains out," I explained.

He said, "She is just bluffing, lock the doors and stay away from the window."

I called my friend Marie; she lived in Berkeley. Albert's apartment was in East Oakland. She said, "Get your ass outta there! When women become emotional like her, they may do anything. Come to my house until Albert gets home."

I called Albert and told him I was going to my friend's house and to call me when he got home. When I got to my friend's house, we waited about an hour. Marie said, "Call her and ask her where she is."

Now you have to think about this because, in those days, we didn't have cell phones or caller ID, so she didn't know I wasn't in the apartment and was actually way across town. I called her.

"Where are you? I'm waiting for you," I postured.

"I decided not to come," she responded.

I said, "Oh, you made a good choice because I was ready to blow your brains out, and don't you dare, as long as you live, threaten me again."

I am such a good bluff. Always have been. I talked a big game, but I have never owned a gun and am too scared to touch them.

My relationship with Albert grew deeper and deeper. We still had problems with his ex. She seemed to have a fatal attraction to Albert. We would go and get his daughter, and no matter what activity or what was bought for her, it was a problem when we returned her. This should have been a warning for me. I would have some rain on my parade. She wouldn't let up and never did. No matter what she agreed to, she would change her mind. Because Albert was awarded the divorce, the judge was very punitive. She decided to withdraw her petition, and the judge accused Albert of not trying to save his marriage. And somehow it all came down to me. His ex was the person who moved out, took everything, filed for divorce, and then wanted to come back. Anyway, this was the first ominous cloud in our beginnings.

Chapter 16: Beginning a New Life Together

     Albert prevailed, but it cost him and us a fortune. He had to pay a large settlement and alimony for a year. Child support was in effect until the child reached the age of 21. I really didn't know how much these things would affect us until after we were married.

     Never think that someone else will think or feel the same way you do. I put myself in her position, and I would never have done the things she did to get him back. Nor would I have used my child as a pawn to do so. Once it was over with me, all I would want from any man was to support his children. I would never keep the children from him, nor tell the children awful stories about him, or compare the children to the bad traits she thought about him. But I soon realized that people don't think like I do. I've never understood how a parent can use their children as bargaining chips. You can't see him or her if I'm angry with you. I think it is the most selfish thing a parent can do.

     When he came home from court, he was so defeated. I felt really sorry for him. He told me he would never get married again. I just listened and smiled. Sometime later, things began to settle. He told me, "My divorce will be final in October."

     "We are going to be married on November 2nd," I announced.

     He said, "Okay."

     Again, I smiled. He bought me an engagement ring, and I tried to kiss him when we came out of the jeweler's, but he was so inhibited and not used to showing emotions in public that I had to wrestle him to kiss me. I was so busy planning our wedding. We agreed to go to Las Vegas and get married.

Does God Have Favorites?

We went to see his mother to tell her we were engaged, and she was definitely not impressed. She didn't comment on my ring at all. She was in the hospital at the time, and her nephew from New York was there visiting. The entire visit he was the main topic of conversation. I was really disappointed that we got that reaction from the first person we told.

We then told Aunt Clara, and Albert told her he bought the cow. She again was not impressed. Aunt Clara was another selfish person and never wanted me to have a family that included Harry because she would lose him. It seemed that when I was happy, the other people and family around me didn't want to share my happiness. My sister-in-law said that my mother-in-law would never accept me. "Why do you think that?" I asked her.

"Because you had a child out of wedlock," she said.

That was not the main reason, but that's what she thought. She was right in some ways. The primary reason was the money she would be losing. Another reason was what her son, Dave, had told her about me. Instead of asking me if I needed anything, like Harry asked, he tried to make a move on me. He got angry with me when I refused to date him in Harry's absence.

My mother-in-law always handled the money. Her husband and sons worked and gave her their money. She became accustomed to this. When Albert was in business and began to give her money right before and after his divorce, she felt that by marrying me, this would stop. She was happy going to her club meetings and having this extra money, and it seemed like old times. I really did try to be a part of the family because I am a family person who was raised to believe and know that family is the foundation. Again, there were walls of doubt and no goodwill toward us getting married. Even his friends and business partners told him it would not work out.

I tried to keep my head above the doubts, whispers, and treatment. I asked God, *Am I going to be disappointed again? Was I again walking into a trap? Would I or could I survive another disappointment?*

I forged ahead and bought a dress, and I had a veil from my friend's wedding as her maid of honor. We decided to drive to Las Vegas and leave after Albert went and said goodbye to his friends in San Francisco. The week that I quit the phone company, I went to the restroom, and I was spotting, not really having a period. I said, "Oh no, not on my wedding day."

My Journey Through Life, Love, and Tragedy

Marie and Albert's friend came with us as witnesses. We were to pick them up so we could leave at 6:30 or 7 pm. I packed my bags and his essentials because I didn't know what suit he was going to wear, so I waited until he came home to put that in the garment bag. I was ready at 4:00 and began to go over everything to make sure we didn't leave anything behind. Six o'clock came, seven, eight, nine, and no Albert. My friend kept calling to ask when we were going. I kept calling his work because he didn't have a cell phone, and he was no longer working there, so even if I got an answer, they couldn't tell me if he was there, and after six, the office was closed. You can't imagine my emotions at that moment. I really began to think I was cursed. I thought, *What had I done to deserve this? Maybe someone has put a hex on me. This couldn't be happening.*

Around 10 o'clock, he comes in, grabs me, kisses me, and says, "Let's go."

"Go where?" I said.

"To get married," he said matter-of-factly.

"If you think I'm gonna start a marriage off like this, you've got anotha thing coming," I fussed.

He acted as if I wasn't talking and took the bags to the car, called our friends, and said we were on the way to get them. He drove for about two hours and finally pulled over, asked me to take the wheel. I did, and it wasn't until I saw him get in the passenger seat and pass out that I realized he was drunk as a skunk and had driven so straight. His friends decided to give him a bachelor party after work, and he never thought of calling me to tell me.

He would often work late or stop by and have drinks, but would not call me. We had a big discussion on this. I told him I was not trying to check up on him, as I think that was the reason he didn't feel he had to call, but it was a matter of courtesy to let me know he was going to be late, and he didn't even have to tell me where he was. I tried to let him know that if I knew he wasn't coming home for dinner or anything else, then I felt free to go where I wanted to go. It didn't seem to set in on him until I turned the tables on him.

After work one day, my friends and I decided to go out, and when he came home, I wasn't there. He panicked, he called everybody, including Aunt Clara, to ask if they had seen me. When I did come home, I asked him how he felt that I had not given him the courtesy of letting him know. It worked. The night we were going to be married, it got out of hand; he had no idea they were going to give him a going-away party. He truly apologized, and believe me, he truly made it up to me.

We got to Vegas and checked into the hotel. Early the next morning, we went and got our license. We then began to shop where we would get married. We decided on the Chapel of the Bells. We made a reservation for 6 PM. We also wanted a minister, and they offered a tape of the wedding vows. They also gave us money to gamble after the wedding. We returned to the hotel, ordered room service, and rested. When we began to get dressed, I noticed my dress was really tight around my stomach. I almost fainted because I knew then I was pregnant. When I get pregnant, it is all in my stomach. I also noticed that after the spotting, I didn't bleed anymore. I told Albert I thought I was pregnant, but he didn't seem to take the news one way or the other. He just said he hoped it was a boy. We got married and went to the casino, where we spent the gambling money, along with champagne. I only sipped a smidgen of the champagne because I thought I was pregnant, and I really don't like alcohol anyway. I won $25, and I was ecstatic because I had been the unluckiest person I knew.

We were supposed to go to a reception that my friend's brother gave us, but I was so tired and did not feel well, so we went to the hotel and went to bed. I felt terrible we didn't go because it seemed he really put on a party, and had an entertainment group come. My friend was also disappointed that we didn't go. But I was exhausted from all the drama of waiting for Albert, the driving, getting a license, making reservations for the wedding, and once it was confirmed that I was pregnant, I knew that it played an important part in my decision. We were supposed to leave the next day.

Albert and his business partner in his now-defunct business had signed to go to Vietnam on a single-status contract. They were paying really good money. He was going to leave four days after the wedding. We went to dinner, and afterwards we played Pokeno. On the way into the restaurant, I joked with the cashier and said we were going to gamble and win a million dollars. She said, "Good luck, and if you do, please take it and go home." We agreed that if we won, we would not play it back but keep it. Albert won $800.00 on the second play. Back then, that was a lot of money. More so because we were really broke. Of course, our agreement almost went out of the window. The house immediately wanted him to play it back, getting five numbers instead of seven or whatever the amount was; they would double his winnings. He got the fever and wanted to do it. When people win, they begin to feel lucky and want to play more. I told him we could go to divorce court before we leave and dissolve the marriage if he didn't take his money.

Preparing for Separation

We went back to the hotel and told our friends our good fortune, and they immediately went but lost a lot of money. I explained to Albert because he kept bugging me about taking 200 and running it up. I said you are leaving for Vietnam, and you have no clothing. You only have suits, shirts, and wing-tip shoes. I needed luggage because I was going to come later. He began to calm down and realized I was right. We decided to get his clothing there because it was hot weather, and so was Vietnam, and clothing in Nevada was always cheaper than in California, though I don't think that is the case now.

We headed home and checked into a hotel in Jack London Square. I began to become nostalgic because he was leaving the next evening from Travis Air Force Base. I think the realization of us being apart was crushing. It had always been us. No matter what the situation, it was us together. We didn't really have a community of support, but we had each other, and I think that laid the foundation for our marriage.

I had ordered a small wedding cake that I picked up the next day. We were going to take it to San Jose so he could say goodbye to his family, and we would share the cake. They didn't really want any of it, so most of it ended up in the garbage. We came back, and I told Aunt Clara to get Harry dressed because I wanted him to ride with me to see his new dad off. She didn't want him to go, but I insisted. I thought it was not only good to show Albert that the three of us were a family, but I also thought Harry would enjoy seeing the planes take off and land. They boarded a big yellow plane. It was not a commercial airliner. I don't know why they would paint an airplane yellow. They took off, and I cried. Harry said, "Don't cry, Mommy." I took him home, and I had made arrangements to stay with a friend from the telephone company until we went to join Albert.

I went the next day to apply for Harry and my passport. I needed my birth certificate. My father was still living, and I asked him if he would go and send it to me. I asked my Aunt Katie to help him navigate the process. He sent me my birth certificate, but it wasn't my birth certificate.

Everything was right except my name. I called him and asked him, "Who is Cora Lois Shannon?"

    He said, "That's you."

    "No. My name is Cora Demetra Shannon," I disagreed.

    "No, it was Lois," he restated.

    I argued, "My middle name is Demetra!"

    "Your middle name is Lois," he insisted.

    All my life, I never knew my middle name was Lois. I didn't find out the story until my oldest sister died. They never told me this because they didn't want me to blab it to my godmother that my mother did not name me after her, as she had promised.

    I bothered my father so much that he finally told me, "Leave me alone. I didn't know you would grow up and go overseas."

    I had to laugh even though I was angry with all of them. I later found out from Lois's daughter that when I was born, the midwife couldn't spell Demetra, and my mother's best friend's name was Lois. She said, "Don't name that child after no white woman. Put my name down."

    You can't begin to know the problem of having to write my name, Cora L. Brown, instead of Cora D. Brown. Every document I have has Demetra or initial D on it. I finally got over that shock, and when I went to apply for our passports, they said Harry had to be on my passport. They couldn't tell me why, except that I would not be able to go anywhere without him. Someone said that people were taking their children overseas and leaving them. I couldn't imagine that, but I didn't intend to go anywhere without him anyway, so both of our pictures were on the passport.

    Albert and I begin immediately to write to each other. I was so lonely without him, and I told him, "I want to come earlier than we planned."

    He said, "Okay. I'll make the arrangements from this end."

    He left in November, and I left at the end of December. Everybody couldn't believe I was going to a country at war with my son, and I was pregnant. I don't think I thought deeply about any of this. I was excited to go to another country and see things I had never dreamed of. I have always been adventurous.

    Aunt Clara was beside herself. She called and did everything she could to keep me from taking Harry. I was not going to leave my child. She didn't understand that I loved Harry as much as I loved life, and I wouldn't do anything to harm him. I was trying to make the three of us a family. She later told me that she had thought of taking Harry to Los Angeles so he wouldn't be there when I came to pick him up. She was desperate.

The End of Life at the Phone Company
I put in my resignation to the phone company. My boss tried to talk me into taking a leave of absence. I told him I was finished with the phone company and would never work for them again. Little did I know they had put on my record never to rehire. I was told by a friend's sister who worked in HR, so that I couldn't put her in jeopardy. I had to let it go. Although I enjoyed some of the years I worked for the phone company, I never thought they would go that far.

It was very fascinating when I started working there. We had to write everything down on these tickets, and we put them into a chute that went to a central desk in the room. The pay phones were the most troublesome. We had to clock the time callers started talking and then go in and tell them, "It is now three minutes. Please deposit the correct amount for more time." Some would comply, and some wouldn't. Some would go to a phone where the release button wouldn't work, and they would accuse us of getting the money. One customer said to me, "You guys should be the richest people in the world, taking all the money from the pay phones."

It was a horrible system because if it were a nickel, we had to mail that amount back to them. We also had places that we would call, in those days, that had a ring-down system.[2] Instead of dialing a number, we could simply lift the receiver (or press a button), which would automatically "ring down" to a predetermined destination—like another operator, a control center, or a specific office. In my case, there was only one operator, and she would have to call another operator in these remote locations. One day, my friend had a call to this remote place in Texas, and she told me to plug in to hear the conversation. The first operator was screaming, "Clare, Clare, can you hear me?"

---

[2] Brown, Evelyn. "Ringdown Phones: Working, Uses & Limitations." *CallWave*, 30 Nov. 2023, callwave.com/ringdown-phones/?utm_source. Accessed 22 Sept. 2025.

Does God Have Favorites?

Clare came on and said, "I've been trying to tell you to stop ringing in my head."

We would fall out laughing at some of the things that happened at the other end. We had to dial everything for the customer. We had all of the downtown San Francisco financial district. Everybody had letter prefixes like Yu2 for Yukon, LA for landscape.

It is amazing how far the phone company and other forms of communication have come. In a way, it is excellent. But what I really miss is that we have lost that human touch. In another way, it's not good when you realize that what you are calling to ask about is not on the phone menu provided. Anyway, I got my last check and went to visit Albert's parents.

Part 9

Life Amid the Vietnam War

Chapter 17: Crossing Oceans, Carrying New Life

During my visit with Albert's parents, I took Mrs. Brown shopping. She wanted some shoes. We went to downtown San Jose, and she picked out these shoes. They cost $40.00. In today's money, those shoes would cost over $380.[3] She didn't thank me, but she said Tiny, her daughter, would get her the purse to go with the shoes. She seemed happy and satisfied, so I let it go.

I was getting ready to leave when Mr. Brown told me he wanted to talk to me. Since I had waited until traffic was heavy, he suggested I stay until it died down. He caught me by surprise. A male parent had never talked to me, and I was scared of what he had to say. He began by telling me,

"Albert is a very complex person. He doesn't think like the average person. His brain is always trying to invent and make money. In doing so, he lacks a lot of the softer things in life and sometimes doesn't consider others in his thinking." He went on to say that Albert was "a good man, and if I could and would stay with him, he would make me a good husband."

At the time, I really didn't understand what he was trying to say until later in our marriage. He was indeed complex, smart, and didn't always think in terms of human thought, but rather in terms of machine language. I was grateful to his father for this wisdom he imparted to me, but most of all that he took the time, which meant he cared about us

---

[3] "Inflation Calculator." *Calculate Me*, H Brothers, Inc., www.calculateme.com/inflation/. Accessed 22 Sept. 2025.

making it. It was also the first time a man had sat and talked to me about life and what I was getting myself into. I will always have fond memories of him. He was such a fine man with good values.

    Harry and I boarded Pan Am to Saigon, now known as Ho Chi Minh City, during the 1960s. We stopped in Hawaii, and I wanted to get out to stretch my legs. Harry had a hard time putting his shoes on because he had taken them off and his feet had swollen. We had a time, and I couldn't carry him because I was pregnant. We finally got off, got some snacks, and returned to the plane. When we got near Ton Su Nut Airport, the plane just dipped suddenly, it seemed a thousand feet. The baby came up seemingly into my throat. When I asked Albert why the plane did that, he said they all did it to avoid artillery fire. I don't know why I didn't get frightened; I just accepted his answer. He was there to pick me up, I had Harry, and baby makes three. I was happy.

    Albert took me to the apartment where he and his ex-business partner lived. It was on the corner of Leloi and Cong Le. It was upstairs over a company that sold something I can't remember. It was also across the street from this nightclub that sang *I Left My Heart In San Francisco* every night. At first, it bothered me, but after listening to it every night, I got used to hearing it. I didn't get used to the smell of Nook mon. I was nauseous for days smelling it. The rooms were huge. Harry had to sleep down the hall, and I was very afraid at first. He wanted to sleep with us. I know he was frightened. It helped that Albert's partner shared the room for a few days before moving out. That eased the fear. Harry was and still is a good child. He makes the most of his circumstances, no matter whether bad or good. We had to go to the USO to use the phone to call the U.S.. You put your name down and wait. We waited all day, and finally they called us to use the phone. We called Aunt Clara first and told her we were safe. I learned later that Harry asked her to come and get him. We then called Albert's mother, and when she heard the announcement of where it was from, she handed the phone to Eddie. I thought we had lost the connection because there was a long pause until I heard Eddie come on and say his mother thought it was bad news, and she couldn't take it. After explaining that we were fine and Albert was fine, she talked. I promised I would write because calling was a hassle. We had Military mail, so it was really reliable.

Gee Hai and the Market

We began to settle into a routine. Our servant's name was Gee Hai, which meant second in the family. She was an older lady, and she admired Harry, so she and Harry would go shopping. They would buy books, toys, and food. She would stand on our balcony with me there and yell, "Yankee go home." She always wore black pajamas, so she may have been Viet Cong (VC). At that time, it was common for South Vietnamese farmers and laborers to wear dark peasant-style clothing. It was just something practical for them to wear. Because it was lightweight, cheap, and readily available, the VC dressed that way so they could blend in with local villagers, making it easier to hide in local communities.[4]

Because of Gee Hai's shouts from the balcony and other behaviors, it seemed that she and others somehow thought we were not Americans. The image of Americans, it seemed, was of blond, blue-eyed people, at least white, if not blue-eyed. The African presence was significant enough that when they had holidays, especially Tết (the Vietnamese Lunar New Year celebration).[5] There were billboard signs featuring an African man showing his teeth and selling Hynos toothpaste. I was surprised and thought *my people are everywhere*. Interestingly, that brand of toothpaste still exists today.[6]

We lived three blocks from the Central Market. It was quite a sight to see all the stalls with merchants selling everything from cloth and meat to medicine and vegetables; you name it, it was there. It was surrounded by vendors selling cooked food. There were also Baychuk drivers to take you where you wanted to go. It was always a game to get one to take me until I began to cry, and then they would laugh, and all of them would scramble to get me into their cart. They would say, "Beau coup," which in French means big. It was always a crowd wherever we went because they had become accustomed to the black male, but to see a black woman,

---

[4] Gaughan, Anthony. "The Faculty Lounge: The Tết Offensive and the Laws of War." *The Faculty Lounge: Conversations about Law, Culture, and Academia*, The Faculty Lounge, 30 Jan. 2018, www.thefacultylounge.org/2018/01/the-tết-offensive-and-the-laws-of-war.html.

[5] Charles Preston Charles Preston is Associate Editor for Religion at Encyclopædia Britannica. "Tết." *Encyclopædia Britannica*, Encyclopædia Britannica, Inc., www.britannica.com/topic/Tết-holiday. Accessed 23 Sept. 2025.

[6] Cam, Saigon Thap, et al. "Anh Bay Cha Hynos." Saigon Thap Cam, 10 Aug. 2020, saigonthapcam.wordpress.com/2020/08 /11/anh-bay-cha-hynos/?utm.

pregnant at that, and a black child, we always drew a crowd. They would really upset Harry by putting their hands on his head and saying in their language, "It feels like steel wool."

Harry would say, "Mama, make them stop."

It was considered rude to make them stop because that was a form of admiration for them. That left me trying to stand between them and Harry, shielding him as much as possible.

Life at the New Martin Hotel

We needed to move, and we were told of the New Martin Hotel. They didn't want us to move there. There was discrimination even in Vietnam. The funny thing about this was that the owner was having an affair with a black enlisted man. He was over the PX and supplying her royally. In Vietnam during that time, the PX (short for Post Exchange) was a major supply hub for American military and civilian contractors. Many local black-market activities revolved around PX merchandise (cigarettes, liquor, electronics, cars, etc.) because those goods were hard to get elsewhere.[7] We were told the owner's husband and children were in San Francisco. Somehow, we moved into the New Martin. Gee Hai packed our things and was very careful so that nothing was taken or broken. She talked to the movers like they were her slaves. We lived on the seventh floor. There was a penthouse above us, and you needed a key to access the elevator to get there. Once we were allowed to go and see it, and it didn't look like it was in Saigon. It was a palace. We had three rooms. One room was the bedroom, and the other room was where Harry slept, and we had a bar where we ate. In between these rooms was the bathroom and kitchen, all in one. The kitchen had a built-in shelf and a sink with storage underneath. On the other side of the room was the toilet and tub. There was no partition between the two. There was no room to put one, even if we had wanted. We cooked on a hot plate. Albert bought an oven with a rotisserie. We put a chicken on the spit, and when it began to turn, Gee Hai went and got every Vietnamese in the building to come and see it. They would watch for hours. It really fascinated them.

I made friends with Tu and her boyfriend, Edward. She also introduced me to her friend Susan. Tu was pregnant as well, but she didn't

---

[7] U.S. Army Center of Military History, "The Post Exchange System," accessed September 30, 2025, https://history.army.mil/html/faq/px.html.

show it. Standing beside me, she looked like the 1960s supermodel, Twiggy. I never knew what Edward did because he didn't wear a uniform, and he didn't work with Albert. Tu would cook spring rolls and fried crab. I would eat until I passed out. It seems strange when I asked for Spring Rolls, here they come out with these cold rolls with shrimp in them. I ask about spring rolls, and they have egg rolls. Spring rolls were made of rice paper dipped in beer and filled with meat and other spices, and fried. Heaven.

    Tu knew enough English to try to interpret for me. She really helped me. I felt sorry for her because Edward couldn't bring her back to the United States. Her brother was inducted into the army. He was only 15 years old. He didn't want to go, and she didn't want him to go, but they had no choice. I never knew what happened to him. There was a beautiful young girl named Bao. She was 13 years old and was being trained to be a prostitute. She and Harry would play on the steps when she could. She really liked Harry, and he liked her. Tu tried to help her. She was sold to this old Vietnamese man, and she ran away. He was not only cruel to her but also wanted to keep her as a slave. She felt that anything was better than being his slave.

    We would all go to dinner on the Mekong Delta, which the Vietnamese call Đồng bằng sông Cửu Long, literally translated "Nine Dragon River Delta,"[8] on boats that sold the best food. We were eating one night, and they told us to all get out. It seemed like an emergency. I asked Albert why, and he didn't want to tell me at first, but I insisted. He said they were checking for charges because they would often blow up the boats. I said okay, and then we were allowed back on to finish our meal. One day, Gee Hai came and said Harry wanted to go home with her, but she told him no because the VC might slash his throat. She didn't say that, but made the gesture of slashing his throat. I told her, "No, no, no. Never take Harry anywhere I don't tell you to."

---

[8] *"Mekong River Delta,"* Encyclopaedia Britannica, accessed September 30, 2025, https://www.britannica.com/place/Mekong-River-Delta.

Chapter 18: Kevin's Arrival

    I was getting bigger and bigger. We were invited to visit Consun Island, the largest of a group of 16 islands located off the southern coast of Vietnam in the South China Sea. It was a place where they kept political prisoners. The beach there was breathtaking. There was another American lady who came and brought her little boy. Harry had someone to play with who was his equal. We all boarded the plane to Consun Island, and we didn't know that General Abrams' photographer was on board, and he took the most beautiful pictures of Harry and Eddie. He also took a picture of Harry playing and being chased by others. It was a perfect day. It brought back memories of peace and quiet. Saigon was very noisy, with the sounds of motorbikes, sirens, people bargaining, and people just living their everyday lives. When we got on the truck to take us back to the airstrip, it took a while to get off the sand onto the asphalt, and when it did, it went way up into the air and came down with a thud. Everybody looked at me because they thought I had sustained an injury. Miraculously, I was ok.

    The most frightening thing that happened to me was on the way back from the doctors. I was riding in this little taxi, trying not to let my feet touch a part of the floor that was rusted out, and something flew into the window and stung me right below my eye. I began to search for blood. I knew I had been shot. My face still stung, but I couldn't feel any blood. On the seat next to me was a leaf. The stem of the leaf came through that window at such speed that it hit my face, and the tip of the stem caused the sting. I couldn't believe that after all the things I should have been afraid of, that really caused me to be frightened.

    I had been recommended to this doctor, who had a clinic and was trained in France. He and I could not communicate except through sign.

Does God Have Favorites?

He could only say, "Zee baby." He was a good doctor. I was getting so tired, and the baby was not dropping, and he did everything to help it along. He would message my suffix, and I would get one or two cramps, but nothing. He wasn't thinking about coming out.

It was becoming close to Tết again, and since the last time they had almost leveled Saigon, they encouraged all of us to get out. We decided to go to Thailand. Everybody said, "Get a guide because they will show you the places off the tourist list." I don't know how we got into this crazy situation, but he was a good guide, except he wanted Albert to get a massage, and you know what that meant. He asked Albert, "Why did you bring her? That's like bringing a ham sandwich to a Luau."

Bangkok was beautiful but crowded, like most Asian cities. They drove like maniacs, and everybody told me that they did. Harry was fascinated by the doorman. He loved to go and pretend he was the doorman. They let him do and play wherever he wanted. Again, his hair was their curiosity. The owner of the hotel asked if Harry could go with him, and I said yes. They didn't bring him back until really late that night. I began to question my sanity. *Why had I let my child go with a stranger?* God is good in that he came back with toys and excitement. So, I know he had a great time, but I did become more cautious. L

In Bangkok, we visited the king's boats.[9] They really weren't boats. They were long, golden barges carved like mythical swans and serpents, glittering in the sunlight. They were magnificent, with hundreds of oarsmen, their paddles rising and falling like wings. It was as if the river itself had become a royal stage. Along with the shops on the riverboats, it was all very exciting. At the time, King Bhumibol Adulyadej, Rama IX, was the deeply revered monarch,[10] so much so that his image was on the walls of shops and temples. In fact, when we went to the movie, we had to stand at the end in respect to the king, as they played their national anthem.

On the last night, our guide took us to a non-tourist restaurant. He said he was going to order for us. I said he couldn't order for me because I am adventurous, but not when it comes to food. I am very picky about my

---

[9] National Museum Bangkok. *Royal Barges National Museum Guidebook.* Fine Arts Department of Thailand.
[10] Handley, Paul M. *The King Never Smiles: A Biography of Thailand's Bhumibol Adulyadej.* Yale University Press, 2006, p. 196.

food. Albert said they could order for him, but they couldn't tell him what it was until he finished. I ordered chicken, and they ordered for Albert. He liked and ate all of it. Then they told him they were Duck feet. I was too tough, but then I remembered that my father used to eat chicken feet, so, except for the web, they were the same. We left and returned home. The Pantells were in Saigon. They were with Foremost Dairy and were showing the Vietnamese how to make ice cream. They didn't leave, and she told me that nothing happened; the flowers and celebration were beautiful.

Rockets in the Night
Little did we know that the VC knew everything we did. They knew when we all got out for Tết, so they decided to launch an offensive when we returned. One night, Ms. Phung called and told us to get our passports and come down to the bar area. She said they were shooting rockets into the city. I tried waking Albert up, but he was out from drinking beer. Beer was 10 cents, and all of the guys would come home and drink beer. I couldn't arouse him, so I went to get Harry and woke him.

"Harry, they are shooting rockets into the city. We have to go downstairs," I told him.

He said, "Mama, I don't want to die."

"Mama isn't going to let you die," I reassured him.

"Okay," he said trustingly.

At the time, I said that I didn't realize the impact of what I had done and said. I had no more power to save him or anyone else. I realized at that moment the trust that children have in their parents. That is why it is so important to love and parent your children to the best of your ability. I realized the passage in Matthew 18:3 of the Bible where it says that you must become like a child to enter the kingdom of heaven. I see what that means now. You must trust and believe in God unquestioningly. Susan took him downstairs, and David asked me to go, and he would bring Albert down. You could hear the explosions. A rocket doesn't give you a warning like a bomb. By the time you hear it, it has exploded. And it comes down from top to bottom, so the lower you are, the safer you are.

We were all crowded in this little bar. We heard hand-to-hand combat outside. The bullets were bouncing off the grills of the buildings. Everybody was afraid. I told one of the girls to turn the jukebox on. I told

Harry to get up on the bar and dance. Harry loved to dance. From a little boy, he loved to dance. He had a babysitter whose grandson taught him to dance, and the two of them would do routines that bordered on professionalism. He said it was me and my shadow. The louder it got outside, the louder I told them, "Turn the jukebox up!" It lasted about 45 minutes. Then it became eerily quiet. It was really stuffy because of the sweat of fear. The military guy who was in there with us came up to me and said, "Thank you."

"For what?" I asked.

"All eyes were on you, and if you had panicked, it would have been pandemonium in there. Because you are pregnant, you are the most vulnerable. Having your son dance took the spotlight off you and what was happening outside," he explained.

I finally got Albert awake enough to take him back upstairs.

"What happened?" he asked. I told him about the attack, and he said, "Next time, leave me upstairs."

"You are insane," I told him.

He agreed the next day after sobering up. I guess it did something to him because he never got that drunk again. The next day was business as usual.

Albert worked in a building not far from where we lived, and one day, as they passed the post office, a bomb blew out the clock. Fortunately, they were on the other side of the street.

Gee Hai, our maid, would use the dish rag to clean the windows, toilet, and anything else she could find. I tried to tell her we had plenty of rags and not to use the dishcloths for anything else but dishes. I even told Tu to try to get her not to use the same rag. She said she quit because I was pregnant, and I was too difficult to get along with. Tu tried to get me another maid, but she couldn't find one.

Zee Baby Arrives

Two days later, I went to the doctor, and he induced labor. I called Albert to bring me my bag, which I had packed, and to come right away. He didn't show until I was well on my way into labor. So, I had the baby in the dress I wore. I also delivered on the examining table with my feet in the stirrups. The baby came after a lot of screaming and the doctor saying, "Zee baby," and I had to keep my feet in the stirrups. I began to think about why I was doing this again. I was in labor for 16 hours with Harry,

My Journey Through Life, Love, and Tragedy

and I promised I would never do this again. My son Kevin was born on July 8, 1969. He was nine pounds eight ounces. He was a beautiful baby, and the nurses couldn't believe he was ours because he was very fair-skinned, and his hair was soft and curly, like most black babies. They didn't understand the genealogy of Black Americans. They didn't know that his grandfather was white with blue eyes. He had one drop of Negro blood, so he was considered Black. It took Albert, Harry, and two Vietnamese to get me off the table onto the stretcher. They took me to my room and took the baby to the nursery. It was hard for me because I didn't have a maid, as was customary with them, to take care of me and the baby. I didn't want to nurse as I should have, so I asked the doctors if he could give me the pills to stop the milk. He said he would, and then he bandaged my breast. This was how they suppressed the milk, and I can't tell you how I cried when I took them off, and my boobs just fell; they had no muscle tone. I had the hardest time getting them to bring me my baby. They would keep him, and I don't know where they would take him, because one day I got really afraid I wouldn't see him again. They kept telling me they were bringing him, and I would wait and wait. I soon began to insist that he stay with me.

    I was finally able to go home. They would not release me for five days. I was worried about Harry because Gee Hai was not there, and I didn't have anybody else. When I got home, I had to wash diapers in the bathtub, and I caused all kinds of alerts. I put them out to dry, and they thought it was a signal of surrender. They came and said I couldn't do that.

    One night, we heard all this racket in the halls and outside the front room window. Tu called and said they were looking for the guy who was having an affair with the owner. It appears that this man was in the U.S. Army and a buyer for the PX, and despite his involvement in black market selling, he decided to purchase a Datsun 280Z sports car. He was riding around in 100-degree heat, in leather gloves, and really showing off. He had an accident with a military vehicle and got out of his car and proceeded to stomp and cuss and really went off. Well, this brought attention to him, and the military began to look at this person and why he was driving around in a sports car anyway. They discovered what he had been doing and where he was staying, rather than staying in the military barracks. They knocked on my door because they were going door to door looking for him. When I opened the door, the soldier and I both looked surprised. A Black woman, a baby in a bassinet, and another child in the other room. I was surprised to see bullets the size of my baby. I had never seen anything that large. He said they were looking for someone, and they wanted to know if he was in our place. I told him no. He asked if he could look through, and I said yes. I think he wouldn't have taken the time if we weren't Black. The man he was looking for was Black, so I guess if he was going to hide, it would be with his people. The only thing we were not his people over there. They finally came down from the roof and got into the apartment. They brought him down handcuffed. I heard they shipped him back to the States. I don't know what happened to his car. I later found out that he had returned to Vietnam after I had left.

After this incident, we had to move again. Before we moved, Tu had her baby. A beautiful baby boy. He had an occidental eye and an oriental eye. I understand his dad brought him back to the States. Tu always said she would give him to the dad because she didn't want him to have the life American children do, especially black ones. She also didn't have any way to take care of him. We moved to an area called Dachai. The building was the tallest in Saigon.[11] It had 11 floors, and we lived on the 11th floor. They used the building to shoot into the city because it rose above everything else. There were bullet holes everywhere. You would think this would have bothered me, but I was just trying to get some place to stay. We moved, and I finally got a maid, but she lasted only two weeks, and I'm happy she didn't last any longer because I found out she had Tuberculosis.

We found out through a friend that another lady was looking for work, and she had been a teacher, but was in disgrace because it was discovered that she having an affair with a married officer. She had been banished. She came to me, and I hired her. She was not the best maid. I think it was because she was not used to being a maid. She really couldn't cook, so I did most of the cooking. I would leave her food. She helped me with Harry. We had enrolled him in Saint Exupery French Vietnamese school. He rode the little bus with the other kids. She knew French, so she could help him with his math and other subjects because I didn't speak

---

[11] U.S. Army Center of Military History, *Tet Offensive 1968*, Washington, D.C.: U.S. Government Printing Office, 1971, 83–85; see also U.S. Military Assistance Command Vietnam (MACV) after-action accounts describing the use of the Dachai Building (Ða Kao) as a defensive vantage point, referred to by U.S. personnel as "the tallest building in Saigon" at the time.

French. Albert was taking French lessons. I think he had a thing for the teacher, but I could never get enough evidence to prosecute him.

We gave Harry a birthday party, and he had six little boys who came. They were from all over the world. He turned seven, and of course, we had ice cream, and our maid knew of a bakery, so he had a cake. The maid was still seeing this man, and she would leave and stay for hours. One day, I put up the food because I didn't want it to spoil, and she announced she was quitting. It took Tu and everybody to get out of her why she was leaving. She said I wasn't pleased with her because I didn't leave her anything to eat. I tried to tell her the food was in the refrigerator, and I only put it there to keep it from spoiling. She was welcome to take anything she wanted from the refrigerator. We finally convinced her to stay, but it was hard. She cried a lot, I think, because she missed her family and position.

Guilt and Grace in a Children's Hospital

Because I didn't breastfeed my baby, I put him on Guigoz[12] milk, a rich French formula. He had cradle cap so bad that I asked around in the American community if anyone knew a pediatrician. I was told to see this doctor at the children's hospital. This doctor was with Doctors Without Borders.[13] I took my baby and came away very depressed after seeing babies lying in cardboard boxes in the hallway—some burned by napalm[14] which is a gelatinous gasoline-based fire-starter that, when dropped, sticks to skin and surfaces, burning at 1,500–2,200 °F. It broke my heart. I was holding my own healthy baby in my arms, beautifully bathed and dressed in all this finery, while theirs were wrapped in bandages, their tiny bodies scarred by a war they didn't choose. I felt guilty. Although I was in a war zone, I never experienced what these poor little babies and people of this country experienced. It was so easy to take certain privileges for granted, no matter how meager they were. There is no question that I had it better than what the Vietnamese were going through.

The doctor told me that Guigoz milk was too rich and contained too much butter, which caused Kevin's cradle cap. I immediately wrote

---

[12] "Guigoz Milk Can." *Vietnamese American Oral History Project, UCLA Digital Library*, accessed 30 September. 2025, https://dal.ucla.edu/vrmc/omeka/s/exhibit24/item/33.
[13] *Vietnam: The Real War*. Associated Press, Abrams Books, 2013.
[14] Ibid.

Aunt Clara and asked her to send me SMA, which stood for Simulated (or Synthetic) Milk Adapted.[15] This milk was one of the first commercially successful infant formulas in the U.S., and from the 1940s to the 1970s, it was heavily marketed as "the formula most like mother's milk." She sent me a dozen cans, and it worked. I told her, and then she sent me so much milk that Albert was bringing home whole milk sacks.

We had Kevin christened at the big cathedral in the square. He looked so large compared to the Vietnamese babies. We had a party and a beautiful cake. There was a bakery in Saigon that would rival any bakery in the U.S.

---

[15] Fomon, Samuel J. *Infant Nutrition*, 2nd ed., W.B. Saunders, 1974.

Part 10

The Journey Back

Chapter 19: It's Time to Go Home

One day, I saw Harry get off the school bus, and I waited for him to come through the door. I began to worry because it was taking too long. Just as I was about to look for him, I heard this voice, "Mama, Mama." I went into the hall, and he was stuck in a dark elevator with no carpet. The elevator had gone above the floor, and there was a little hole through which he could see me. I told him, "Mama is here. We'll get you out."

Albert went downstairs to see if anyone was there, and he found them sleeping. He got them up, and they told him that they would come when their nap was over. The next thing they knew, they were being dragged up the steps. Albert said, "You are going to get my son out of this elevator!" They went to the roof, and we later found out that it was out of oil. They put oil in it and started cranking it, and when they did, the elevator started down, and all I could hear was "Maaaaaaaa." Albert was going down with it, and when they reached the lobby and the door opened, they walked up 11 flights of stairs. From then on, poor little Harry had to walk. I didn't want him to get stuck again.

My baby was growing and needed care, and the doctor who helped me before had left and gone to another site. The doctor she referred me to didn't really want to help me because he felt the other babies were more in need, and I felt that way also. I told Albert I thought we should go home. They had also closed the PX to contractors, so we had to rely on the local market, which was not good. Tu tried to talk me out of leaving and said she would shop for me, and she knew a meat shop where I could get meat. She didn't want me to go. Most of the expats were eating at the Circle Sport T,[16] a French club that they offered us to join, but I refused to join a

---

[16] Neil Sheehan, *A Bright Shining Lie: John Paul Vann and America in Vietnam* (New York: Random House, 1988), 294–296.

club that wouldn't allow the citizens of their own country to be members. They could work there, but they could not join. That was ludicrous. They had an outbreak of hepatitis, and it all stemmed from that club. He had two months left on his contract, but another company wanted him to stay for another six months. I really didn't want him to stay that long, so he signed up for four months instead.

Wrapping Things Up and Leaving Saigon
We prepared for the children and me to go home. I really didn't want to leave Albert. I wanted us to come home together. This would be another separation, but it was necessary. Albert was going to move in with another guy because he didn't need all the space we had at this apartment. So, we broke up housekeeping, and the maid asked if she could have certain items. I was happy to give them to her. I had to write her a note stating that these items were given to her by me. She said if they stopped her and she could show proof, if she couldn't, they would take them and say she stole them. She rode with us almost to the airport. She asked to be let out at the destination she wanted. I often wondered what happened to her. I have wondered about all the people we knew in Vietnam. I know Edward came home and brought his son. He lived in Baltimore, I think. I once had his number, but when I moved, I lost track. Albert's ex-business partner came home and brought a family of Vietnamese with him. He set them up in a restaurant business in Palo Alto. We went to it, and it brought back memories. Dave and Susan got married and came back. I never knew where they lived. Albert fired Dave, which led to bad blood between them. I don't know what happened to Harry's little friend whose mother worked there. I think they left around the same time as I did. There was a man who worked in Albert's office who told stories all day. They wanted to fire him, but the office people said they would take away their fun and amusement. He told preposterous stories. He said the Queen knighted him. They told him he was not an English citizen, and he would say they made a special exception for him. He smuggled teak by swimming miles, he said, and invented a machine that added zero time. He was a character and entertaining. He told only lies about himself, so he was harmless to me.

The last person I remember ended tragically. Mr. Houk wanted to come to the United States so badly. He had us for dinner one night, and it was my first time using a Vietnamese toilet. You had to put your two feet in stirrups on each side and squat to use the toilet. You can't imagine how

My Journey Through Life, Love, and Tragedy

I felt, pregnant with all this weight. That was an experience I will never forget. Mr. Houk made it to the States and had a heart attack when he landed. That really broke my heart. He was such a nice man.

Turbulence Over Water

We flew out of Saigon, and my first stop was Hong Kong. We experienced so much turbulence that everybody thought the plane was going down. They had everyone return to their original seats. Harry had gone up front and was talking to someone, and he had to come back. Kevin never woke up in my lap. I guess the turbulence rocked him to sleep. We were over water and I was really frightened. I hate water, and I could see us drowning or being eaten by a shark. I told Harry, "If we go down, you hold onto me and don't let go," trying to mask my fear.

"Mama, what about Kevin?" he asked.

"I am going to tie him to me," I reassured him.

We rocked and rolled for almost 30 minutes. My nerves were raw when we landed. I lived in Saigon for two years, and I was never as afraid as I had been on that plane. We stayed in Hong Kong for three days. Jackie, a Vietnamese woman, went with us to Hong Kong on a shopping trip. She was married to a Black American male who was really a nerd in the greatest sense of the word. I never knew what he did. He was probably a CIA agent because he certainly acted like one. Albert had met him through the other expats, and when he found out we were leaving to go home, he asked if she could go with us to Hong Kong. We checked into the hotel, and I was exhausted from the day and mostly from the plane ride. We all showered and fell asleep. The next day, we visited the Hong Kong side of the Tiger Balm Garden.[17] It was unlike anything I had ever seen — a vibrant collection of statues, dragons, and three-dimensional life-sized scenes that made Disneyland look tame. It was beautiful. Sadly, much of it was demolished in the late 90s to make way for luxury housing. Harry liked riding the ferry.

I hired an *amah* (a Chinese woman who served in the role of babysitter or household helper) to sit with Kevin. We went shopping, and Jackie wanted to have a Chinese dress made. I wanted one also. She found

---

[17] Sinn, Elizabeth. "Aw Boon Haw's Tiger Balm Gardens: Commerce, Morality and Chinese Modernity." *Journal of the Hong Kong Branch of the Royal Asiatic Society*, vol. 45, 2005, pp. 1–28.

this tailor, and we both picked out our material. When he told her the price, it was double what he had wanted to charge me. I asked, "Why does my dress cost more than hers?"

"Because she is Chinese," he answered.

"I don't want you to make me a dress," I decided.

"I'll give you the same price. I know how *your people* (blacks) are treated in the U.S."

I couldn't believe he knew more about our plight than some of my own people. The next day, we picked up our dresses and continued shopping. I was looking at these beautiful pictures when a Black man came in and began to ask where I lived. He said he would buy me the picture and have it shipped for me. I told him, 'Thanks, but I would buy it.' He insisted, and then I couldn't get rid of him. I told him that my friend and I were supposed to meet her friends in an hour, and I would have to go. He asked when I was leaving, and I said the next day, which was the truth. I felt uncomfortable with someone hitting on me. I didn't consider myself single anymore, and I was in the motherly mode. He finally left, and I never got my picture. He probably went back and canceled it. I bought Harry a wallet and he was so excited. We took the ferry later that day, and someone picked his pocket. We had been warned about pickpockets. Harry cried because I didn't have enough to buy him another one. I promised I would when we got home. We left the next day for home, and I prayed and prayed that our flight would be better than the last one. It was.

Chapter 20: A Different Kind of Homecoming

We finally landed in San Francisco. Aunt Clara and Uncle Horace broke through the line and came and got the children before I could finish customs. I had so many dirty diapers that they just let me go through. It felt surreal to be home again.

When we lived in the New Martin Hotel, the street next to it was Tudo Street. It was the Miracle Mile of Saigon. I had gone over and purchased two beautiful ceramic elephants. Actually, I had them on layaway. I gave Albert the papers and asked him to please pay and ship them to me. They were going to be my base for a cocktail table. They were all hand-carved and the best. After being home for about a month, I got these elephants. I knew they weren't the ones I purchased because they were too tall. They were elephants that you could get in any marketplace. I was so angry with Albert. Aunt Clara said, "Be glad he sent you anything." I just looked at her. Just because she took all the mess from Uncle Horace didn't mean I was going to be that kind of wife.

Albert and I communicated by sending each other tapes. It was so funny to feel afraid for him because when I was there, it was just routine. Now that I was thousands of miles away, hearing and reading about Saigon, it was all different, and again I questioned my sanity.

Harry Takes His Stand

Before we left for Saigon, Harry and the boy next door got into a fight. Whenever anything happened that Harry didn't like, he would run in and tell Aunt Clara. She would go out and get his toys and tell the kids to go home. Albert saw it once, and when we left to come home, he told Harry, "You have to be the man until I get home. If I hear about you running from the kids or a fight, I'm going to clean your clock when I come home. Understand?"

Harry said, "Yes."

We were home a week, and the fight started again. Again, he came in the house muttering and saying he wasn't going to play with him, and Aunt Clara began to go into her usual action. I stopped her.

"Do you remember what your dad told you before we left Saigon?" I reminded him. He turned around, went back out, and began to lay into this boy. He beat him until we told him to stop. He was acting out of fear. We didn't have any more fights or disagreements. Everybody had a new respect for themselves and each other.

When I first returned from Vietnam, we enrolled Harry in school. I wanted to put him in the French American School, but it was located in San Francisco, which presented a problem. I found a teacher for him to continue his French. After about six months, she persuaded us that we were wasting our money because Harry had no one to speak French with except her. So, we stopped the lessons.

Settling Back in the Neighborhood

Most days, I visited Marie, who lived not too far from my aunt. She was a marvelous cook and could cook the most delicious pork chops, my favorite, in the world. She would cook her husband's dinner, and I would have to go to the store. She would end up cooking him some more because I would eat mine and his, too. I would cause a scene because I wore my Vietnamese dress almost every day. They are very comfortable.

I began to look for a place for us to live so that when Albert came home, we would have a home. I found this cute duplex in Oakland, and we moved in. It didn't have a refrigerator, and I didn't have the credit to buy one. My sister-in-law let me use her Sears account to buy one. We had a crib for Kevin, a twin bed for Harry, and a double for Albert and me. We didn't have a dining table; we only had a sofa and one chair. The place was really nice. It had a large, fenced-in backyard for the kids to play, and the lady who lived in the front unit was the cousin of my friend Pat. She had my dog. A friend had given me a poodle, and I really wasn't supposed to have animals in my apartment. One day, I went to visit my friend. She was ill with cancer, and I took Cognac with me. I brought her in with me, and she immediately got into the bed with her. I didn't mind because I didn't want her running around the house. When I got ready to leave, the dog would not come with me. I tried to get her, and she growled at me. My friend said, 'Leave her.' I did, and I had mixed feelings about it. For once, I really liked this dog, and then she took him off my hands so I wouldn't have to move, which consoled me knowing he would have a good home. My friend died when I moved to New York. Four years later, when I moved into this place, Pat's cousin had the dog. Her father married my friend, and when she passed away, she left the dog to her. I was quite surprised to see it.

Almost Dying, New Jobs, and Moving Again?
Albert came home, and it was short-lived. He interviewed with Ross Perot's company, and they hired him. He called me to come and pick him up. We were using an old Cadillac of his dad's, and when I went to pick him up, a tire blew out, causing it to spin me around and face the wrong way on the freeway. People stopped to see if I was hurt, and I was able to pull the car to the side of the freeway. A highway patrolman came and let me use his car radio to call dispatch, so they could call my sister-in-law to see if she could pick me up and then go and pick up Albert. It was hours before we could get him, and when we did, he was livid. He didn't seem to care that I was almost killed.

Like I said, Albert would react sometimes in the craziest way. I think he was going through culture shock, and I really realized it when he took the money that was offered. I asked him how we were supposed to live off that small amount of money? It wasn't even half of what he was making. I knew we wouldn't be paid the same as when we were in Saigon, but this was ridiculous. Perot had a policy that you could not mention or discuss your salary, and if you did, that was cause for dismissal. I can see why, because you didn't know where you stood in comparison with someone of your status. We had paid off every bill he and I owed when we were in Saigon. We came back owing nobody but completely broke. He had bills from his company to pay, and with child support and alimony, we were flat broke. We had his last paycheck to live off. So, I later thought he was under immense pressure.

Albert couldn't stand not working. He had a great sense of responsibility. It wasn't a week before they said they were sending him to New York to work. We had just been back together for a week, and now we were going to be apart again. He said he would go and get a room until we could save some money. I again saw him off. I began to think we were going to have a long-distance marriage forever. I applied to IBM and was hired as a dispatcher. I was to start in a week.

One morning, I was awakened by someone trying to open the front door, and I turned over to go back to sleep, because in my mind, I thought it was Albert coming home. I realized Albert was in New York. I immediately got up to discover that a man had broken into the house. When I heard him, he was trying to get out of the house. He was running down the driveway, so I only saw the back of his head. The scary thing was that he had come in through the window where my children were sleeping. Kevin was awake and standing in his crib, but Harry never woke up. I always sleep with a window open. I really get claustrophobic when I can't get fresh air. I would sometimes freeze Albert to death with my open window. The thing that bothered me the most was that the intruder was in the room with my children, and he could have killed them and me too. I was really shook up. I called my brother, and he came and nailed the window shut. I was still uncomfortable. I didn't know what to do. I didn't want to stay there, and I didn't want to leave and give up my job. They were paying a good wage, and we could get ahead much faster if I stayed. My longing for Albert won out. I called IBM and told them I wouldn't be starting because I was moving. They were not too happy. I decided to go to New York.

Part 11

From New York to California and Back

Chapter 21: Finding a Home in New York

Albert's company paid for me to come and find a place to live. Aunt Clara threatened not to keep the boys. She knew we were taking Harry away again. After threatening to leave them with a friend, she relented. Albert had a cousin who lived in Harlem, and knew their cousin Sharon from Wichita. Albert was born in Wichita. Sharon and her husband lived in LeFrak City in Queens. I knew nothing about New York except that it had a garment industry that I always wanted to see. His cousin, who lived in Harlem, thought LeFrak City was the place. I think they had recently let Blacks move into it. I was not impressed at all. The first floor was the basement. The walls were cement, and I know you are going to think this funny, but living in Saigon among all those masses of people, I was comfortable, but in New York, I was frightened. I can't explain it. New York always scared me. The people are rude and never seemed to know or want to know you. They were very impersonal. His cousin couldn't believe I wasn't impressed with this LeFrak City.

Someone at Albert's work got in touch with a realtor in Long Island. Her name was Candia, and she and I became friends. She really went to bat for us. Port Washington, Long Island, New York, was located at the end of the Long Island Railroad. It was a very rich community. We were truly out of our league. They had a wonderful complex that I asked if we could apply there, and Candia said that the complex was built for the servants who worked on that Island. They were descendants of servants who had come long ago to work, and each generation stayed, with a built-in job available if they wanted one. She said we didn't qualify to live there. She said there was a place on Manhasset Blvd. she wanted to show us. We really liked it, but the owner turned us down because we were Black. We met the required qualifications, and there was no reason not to rent to us. Because he was running for political office, Candia threatened to expose him if he didn't rent to us. She had him in the crossfire, and he decided he'd rent it to us. I returned home to pack and prepare for the move. He later had the realty board fine her for unethical practices. I just couldn't believe it. It was not unethical not to rent to us, but for her to make him do the right thing was unethical. Being a Black person in the world and especially in the United States is very deflating at times. We are always challenged, and we have to prove ourselves to be worthy of white people's whims and wants. I can see why we die earlier with heart and other diseases because of always being in a state of anxiety. We are always at the mercy of the master.

Pots, Pans, Police, and a Proposition

Before I left New York, I went to Abraham and Strauss to buy some pots and pans so Albert could try to fix some simple meals. It was and is very expensive to live in New York. I cooked dinner and breakfast for us while I was there. On the way to get the cookware, I walked because I didn't trust the bus. It wasn't that far, nor was it that close, but I was young and didn't mind walking. On the way there, I was approached by the police. My heart almost stopped.

They asked, "Could you show us your ID, ma'am?"

"Why?" I asked.

"You look like someone we're looking for," they replied.

I showed them my ID, and the information didn't match. I asked them, "Why was I stopped?"

"You look like Angela Davis," they answered.

"I look like Angela Davis?" I mused.

"Yes, you do."

"Do you think I would be out in the open in New York if I was Angela Davis with the whole country looking for me?" I confronted.

"Sorry, ma'am. We don't know what she would be thinking, but you can go," they concluded. And I was surprised they apologized. I couldn't believe it.

I got the cookware, and it was really heavy. This guy saw me struggling with it and came over to take it from me without asking. I thought, *Oh my God, this person is going to steal this cookware.* He said he would walk me home and carry it for me. I felt I had no other choice but to accept since he already had it in his hand. We get to the apartment, and he wants to come up. I told him he could not do that, and I then realized what his intentions had been all along. I can be dense at times when it comes to understanding people's intentions. I think the doorman asked him to leave because he saw that he wasn't going to let me go. I was very appreciative after that. I tipped him that time.

A Lesson in Tipping

Tipping a doorman was something I wasn't used to. When I first came, Albert would tip him, and he was anxious to open the door. I tipped him once after that because I had packages, but when I didn't tip him, he would turn his back to me when I entered. I asked Albert, "Why did he do that?"

Albert said, "He expects you to tip him every time you go and come back."

"Well, I can open the door myself," I mentioned.

After I told Albert and his cousin my experience with the man who "helped me" with my cookware, they both admonished me, "Never, I mean never let anyone take your packages, let alone find out where you live."

Another rude experience I had in New York was at the airport.
I tipped the skycap, and he asked, "Ma'am, where are you going?"
"California," I told him.
"I hope you stay there until you learn how to tip," he quipped.
"Give me back my tip if it wasn't enough!" I postured.
Of course, he didn't.

Chapter 22: Cross Country Road Trip

I was so happy to get back to California. I missed my children and was anxious to get back to start our life in Port Washington, Long Island, New York. Marie had a friend who owned a car dealership. I wanted a new car, but I didn't have the credit or the down payment. I let him talk me into this Opel Kadett. It was a stick shift, but I didn't mind; I learned to drive using a stick shift. I really didn't want to drive to New York by myself. I thought of my old friend from Berkeley High. She had sent her book to a publisher in New York and was waiting for an answer. She was really anxious to hear something from them. She said she would ride with me if I would pay her way back. I told her I would, but she would have to stay at least two weeks because it would take that long for Albert to turn in his expenses and get them back. I reemphasized this to her, and she said, 'Okay.' Oh boy, what a nightmare.

We packed the car. We had a spare tire, and we had the car serviced. Harry and Kevin were in the back seat, among many other things, because this was a small car, and our furniture and other things would take at least three weeks to deliver. The trunk was so packed that you couldn't even fit a piece of paper in it. I picked her up and we started out. I am a seasoned traveler. Uncle Horace and Aunt Clara drove to Memphis three times while I lived with them, and Uncle Horace had a plan about driving. He would try to cover 800 miles a day, but he always insisted on getting sleep, rest, and a shower at the end of the day. It really renewed your ability to drive more alert and longer. We hadn't gotten out of California before my friend began to complain.

"Could we just please stop and get a hotel? I promise I'll ride longer tomorrow. I just really need to sleep," she begged.

I gave in, but I was also on a budget, as well as short on time. We got up the next morning, and it would take her longer to get dressed than all three of us. We always had to wait. We would go and get breakfast and head out. I'm doing the driving, and she is eating and singing. The next night wasn't too far before the singing started, and we stayed at the state line of Nevada. The next day, we started out, and I was determined to get to Cheyenne, Wyoming. We had lost a lot of time, and I was going to run out of money if we stopped this often. We had gotten within 30 miles of Laramie, Wyoming, and it was dark, but I was determined to get to Cheyenne. We had a flat tire, and I had to pull over on the shoulder. When I got out, the wind was whipping rock and debris everywhere. My friend never got out, and I didn't want or expect the boys to get out. So, I started unloading the trunk to get to the tire, when, as we say, God sent a ram in the bush. A white family stopped and asked if we needed help. I said I thought I could handle it, and he said they really didn't mind. He and his son finished removing all of the stuff from the trunk and the tire. They were going to take the flat tire off when he asked, "Do you have a lug wrench?"

"Never thought of that. I don't think I do," I wondered.

"Let me see if mine'll fit." He was in a big Chrysler, and again I was saved because he had a 4-way wrench. That meant he had one small enough to fit my tire. They finished, put all the stuff back, and placed the tire on top so that it would be easy to access when we arrived at a station to fix it. "Where're you headed?"

"Cheyenne," I answered.

"I wouldn't try to get there tonight, but try to get to Laramie. It's only 30 miles. And I wouldn't want you to have another tire or other car problem in the middle of the night," he strongly recommended.

The Long Drive East

I took his advice and stopped in Laramie. We found the cutest, coziest little motel I've ever seen. We all got settled, and after listening to the news, it was reported that they were expecting snow. When I awoke the next morning, I called the Highway Patrol to ask about the weather, and they told me that it was snowing in Laramie. If I started now, I should be able to outrun it and make it to Cheyenne, where it wasn't snowing yet. I began to throw things together to get out of there, and then I yelled at the boys because they were playing in the snow instead of helping me pack the car. I might as well let them play because by the time my friend got through putting on organdy blouses and makeup, the snow had begun to stick.

    We finally got on the road, and I got on Highway 80 and must have hit black ice. I began to spin, and I tried all the things I had been taught in driver training. To not put your foot on the brake too hard and turn into the spin, and that didn't work, and I tried turning opposite the spin, and that didn't work, and I finally let go of the wheel because I lost control and let whatever was going to happen, happen. We landed in the ditch that divided the highway. I was happy we went that way instead of the cliffside. When we stopped, I sat to try and compose myself, and my friend was praying, "Help us, Jesus." I started the car, and the back wheels were mired in mud, and I couldn't get traction. My friend began to protest and said we should just wait until someone came along. I told her I was not going to stay there and let me and my boys freeze. There was nothing I could put under the wheel to get traction. Again, I learned in Driver's Ed how to rock the car back and forth until I could get out of the rut. It was easier since I had a stick shift. We finally gained enough traction to get back on the highway, and I stopped under a viaduct to stop shaking and calm down. A snowplow came along, and I immediately followed it until we began to clear the snow. I would shift now and then to avoid wearing out one gear. I was going slowly, but we finally got into Cheyenne. We found a station that had a restaurant adjacent to it. I had my friend and boys go in and order while I dealt with the tire. They said it would be $125.00 for the tire.

    This was in 1971. I had no choice but to pay for it. I often wondered if it was because I was a Black woman alone or if they had to get the tire from another dealer. In that part of Wyoming, small cars are not that prevalent. Most cars are large and have 4-wheel drive. Anyway, that really put a dent in my budget. We ate breakfast, but I wasn't very hungry, so I didn't order a large stack of pancakes, unlike my friend. She was never concerned about any of the events happening to us or around us. I don't know if she didn't feel it was her problem, that she was just there to keep me company, or what. I once asked her to drive because I was so tired, and she said she really didn't feel comfortable driving.

    The next night, we stayed in Lincoln, Nebraska. I didn't realize how swollen my legs were until I took a shower and tried putting on lotion, and it began to sting. It was from the night I had stopped for the flat tire. We started the next day with the intention of stopping in Rockford,

Does God Have Favorites?

Illinois, where my sister Marion lived. This was supposed to be a retreat for a couple of days, allowing the boys to stretch, play, and get out of the car. My sister spoke to Mary, and she seemed to have gained their confidence to be against me. I don't know if it was Marion's teaching of always treating a guest well or what. We would get into a discussion, and it seemed that Marion and Mary were on the same side, and I was the odd person out. To add insult to injury, my brother came over from Chicago and commented, "You came across country in that."

"Yes," I said. "And I'm going to New York in that."

I may have a complex, but it always seemed I was never encouraged or praised for doing or trying anything. Other people always said nice things about me, but my family always seemed to find ways to put me down. All the weather, driving, and facing the unknown with two young children, I would have been proud that someone would be brave enough to try to reunite their family. It was always a downer. It was time for us to go the next day, and Mary asked if I would mind if she stayed with my sister. She was being praised for her accomplishments and what she did, and her ego was over the moon. I told her I couldn't make her continue with me, but she would have to go home on her own.

I called Albert from my sister's and told him we had made it to Marion's and when we would be leaving. If all went as planned, we would or should be there not later than two days. He said he would be waiting for us. I got up and began packing and getting the car ready, and Mary said she would continue with us. I was conflicted with her decision. I needed another person, but other than being in body, she was of no help to me.

I drove from Illinois to the beginning of the Poconos in Pennsylvania. I was so tired, but I was determined to get to New York. I was running out of money and had only enough to buy gas. I stopped at a lodge, which had a restaurant. I went in to get coffee to try to keep myself awake. The coffee was served at the bar along with the other drinks. While getting coffee again, a white man asked me where I was coming from and where I was going. I told him I had stopped in Illinois and was going to New York. He said you plan to go to New York tonight. I said yes. He asked, "Have you ever driven through the mountains before?"

"Yes. In California," I answered.

"The Poconos are a different story. I suggest you stay here and start afresh in the morning," he recommended. "If you don't have the money, I'll pay for the room."

My Journey Through Life, Love, and Tragedy

"My children and my friend are in the car," I informed him.

"You go and get them because I really, in good conscience, can't let you make that drive during the night," he advised.

I was again conflicted. I really didn't know or trust his motive. I didn't see why he was so concerned and willing to pay for someone he didn't know. I told him I could pay, and we would stay. I asked Mary if I could borrow the money from her until we got to New York, and I would give it back to her right away. She agreed reluctantly. Mary is very tight with her money and everything else about her. Very secretive, and unless you are flattering her, she doesn't have too much to say. We stayed the night, and again, she paid for breakfast for the first time.

We left and headed for New York. The scenery in the Pocono Mountains was breathtaking. We finally got into New York City. We didn't know where to get off the highway. We only knew the address where Albert was staying in Manhattan, and the number was low. We got off in the hundreds, but I knew that if we stayed on this street, we would eventually reach the street he was on. We finally got there after fending off people trying to wash our windows and do other things to the car at the light for money.

Chapter 23: Life in New York

Albert was at work but had left word with the doorman to let us in. We parked in the garage across from the apartment. It was $35.00 for one night, and they made it plain they were not responsible for anything left in your car. I just prayed no one would break in and take our belongings. We could only take so much with us across the street. Albert would come later and get the other things, but we had to trust that it would still be there before he came. The apartment was beautiful. We were across from the Chrysler Building. The company was paying $135.00 a day for this place. When he finally got home, we were all over him, and all of us were so happy.

Hopes Deferred

My traveling friend immediately called the publishing company, but was unable to reach them. We were to move the next day to Port Washington. She called them again, and they rejected her book. She was really no good after that. We packed the car going back and forth three or four times until we had everything in it. We had to take Albert's stuff also because he was coming later on the train. I was amazed that I remembered how to get there, but we made it. Candia had gone and rented us bedding and had all the beds made up with clean sheets, comforters, and pillows. She also had stocked the refrigerator with food for at least three to four days. She had sent Albert the keys, so all we had to do was move in. The boys had to sleep together because they had twin beds. My friend slept in the other one.

I picked Albert up from the Long Island Expressway, also known as the L.I.E., and we were ecstatic to be together. I was so tired of being anxious, driving, and dealing with everything that happened along the way; I just wanted to sleep, but I was too keyed up. We finally all slept. I got up and took Albert to the train station. Candia told me which school to go to and register Harry. It was the Guggenheim School, and Harry was the only Black child in the school. When we came back from the registration, my friend had packed her bags and said, "Cora, I'm going home."

"Why?" I asked.

"I feel like I don't belong. When your family all hugged and kissed, I felt left out."

"We just moved here, so I don't know how to get to the airport," I informed her. "And don't forget, I don't have your money yet," I reminded her.

I gave her the money I borrowed, but I didn't have the money to buy the ticket. We had been there for a total of three days, and I hadn't had time to gather all the receipts and give them to Albert to submit with his expense report. My friend was inconsolable. She insisted on going home.

Candia came to get me to go and sign some papers, and she was going to take us to lunch. My friend didn't want to go with us. At this point, her mind was made up. We went and took care of business, had lunch, and picked up Harry from school. When I returned home, my friend was gone. She took a taxi to the airport and bought a ticket. She claimed she had paid one-half of the ticket, with the rest due in 30 days. I have never heard of that, but I didn't challenge her; I just accepted what she said and reassured her that I would have her money at that time. Unfortunately, Albert didn't file his expenses when he should have, and 30 days came and went. She would call every day and pressure me about the money. I was almost tempted to borrow it from someone to get her off my back. He finally got his expense check, and I sent her the money. She never called again while I was in New York.

Changing Jobs and Houses

Life began to settle somewhat. I became involved in Harry's school. I became a Den Mother. He had a friend named Andrew, and he was so hyper that he had to take medication. Albert got another job and was paid much more than he was making at EDS. He gave his two weeks' notice and was ready to start this other job. They called and said he had claimed to have graduated from Golden Gate University, but they couldn't find any record of him having done so. Now, he's out of work, and I'm not working.

So, I went to work at North Shore Hospital in the personnel office. I had the funniest boss, and everything I said or did made him laugh. I really liked working there. We received a large IRS return, which kept us afloat until Albert got a job back at Honeywell in Framingham, Massachusetts. That meant another move. Albert went first and was supposed to find an apartment. We were to come after he got the apartment. We gave notice, packed the car, and set out for Framingham. I learned the day before Kevin had mumps in one jaw, so we had to be careful. When we arrived, we went to look at the apartment, and I can't even begin to tell you the disappointment I felt. It's so funny, all during our marriage, I was able to depend on the one thing that Albert does well, and with thought, and that is work, especially with computers. The bedrooms were so small you couldn't get a double bed in them. We had a king-size bed. The living room and a space the size of a closet for the dining room table. There wasn't anything dividing the kitchen. When you walked into the living room, the kitchen, and the eating area were in the space that had been my living room in the apartment we had left. The clincher was the bathroom. The window was painted red so no one could look inside. It was also located in an area where there were no Black people. It was bordering where the Irish lived, and they hated Blacks. I discovered why that history went back so far. I told Albert we could not live there. I called the realtor and told her the apartment was not adequate. She suggested I get a double bed to accommodate the bedrooms. I told her I would not and that the window in the bathroom would definitely have to be replaced. After haranguing with her, she finally agreed to give me back my money.

I can't remember how we found out about Framingham and Adele. We went to see her the next day, and she found us an apartment with a basement. It was more expensive than the other one, but it was worth it. We moved into this apartment with a 1-year lease. It had three bedrooms, a separate dining room, a large eat-in kitchen, two bathrooms, and a full basement that I wanted to fix for the children to play. We were extremely broke when we moved because we were coming off a period of Albert not working. It seemed that for every month you don't work, it takes a year to get even. Candia and her family came to visit. Her aunt and uncle lived in

Does God Have Favorites?

Boston. Her uncle was an ambassador under John F. Kennedy. She took Albert to Boston with her, and he was so impressed with their house. I couldn't imagine him being impressed with any house after finding that box he wanted to live in. Albert's cousin Sharon and her husband also came to visit, and we had a wonderful time. Sharon was so much fun. She was much younger than me, but we really hit it off. I loved her laid-back attitude. I suppose that when I first started and didn't have as much responsibility, I was like that, at least I hope I was. The electric bill was horrendous. The apartment was all heated with electricity. It didn't seem that the walls were very well insulated, as it was hard to keep them warm. We were really struggling to make ends meet.

Harry's Boots

We bought Harry a pair of boots for the snow, and we told him he could not lose them because we had no more money for any more. The next day after school, we got a call from his teacher, saying that Harry had hit this kid for no reason. We knew immediately that it was not true. We never had any trouble with Harry in school or any other activity where he participated. He was a pacifist. We made an appointment to meet. We also told the teacher that that behavior was not Harry's and we wanted her to talk with both boys and find out what really happened. We went to the school the next day, and an apology was made to us and Harry. It seems this kid had taken Harry's boots and wouldn't give them back. He threw them, and when Harry tried to retrieve them, he would get them and throw them again. Harry asked him to stop, and the thought of him coming home without those boots was too scary. He tried to stop the kid when he was about to throw the boots, but instead, he hit Harry with them. Harry returned the favor. But when they called, they acted like Harry was a terrorist. Again, Harry is the only Black kid in the class, and there weren't that many in the school.

Almost Perfect Housing

The bills and electricity got so high that I called Adele and asked her to look for us a house with a rent-to-buy option. She said they were very hard to come by, and I told her I knew that that was why I was asking her now, so by the time our lease was up, we would be able to negotiate. Adele came back two months later with a house with a rent-to-buy option.

She was as surprised as I was. I asked her what I could do about breaking my lease. She said she would talk to our landlord and explain our situation. He asked me to call him. I did, and he said he would let me out of my lease if I left my deposit. I told him I would. So we started the negotiation to get this house. It was at 51 Winter Park Rd., not very far from where we lived. The street was shaped like a horseshoe. You could enter the street in two ways and leave without going into another street. It was perfect for kids because no one came down the street except the people who lived there and sometimes visitors. On the other side of the street, their yard bordered a military hospital. This little house was the worst-looking house on the street. I found out that there were some investors who sold custom-built homes. They ran out of money and sold the remaining lots to another investor. This investor came in and put up three-bedroom, one-bath homes on lots that were scheduled for much bigger houses.

    Our backyard, without exaggeration, could have accommodated a swimming pool and tennis courts, or an in-law quarters, and still have land to barbecue. The person who owned the house was divorced and had rented it out. The people renting left without notifying the owner. The house had what they call radium heat. It was built on a slab, and the copper pipes were embedded in the floor. It was heated with oil. When the oil ran out, the pipes froze, and unless you tore up the entire flooring in the house, there was no way to repair it. The owner discovered that the pipes from the heating unit, which ran under the door in the living room, were open. So, he installed baseboard heat, starting where he could attach the pipes to the baseboard. The only problem with this was that once he started, he had to run the baseboard all around the house, through every room, making the rooms extremely hot. The screen door was on with a rope. It had gray institutionalized tile floors. It had a cute corner fireplace. A dining area right outside the kitchen. It had one bathroom. I thought it was the most beautiful house in the world because it was going to be my first house. I went to Sears and purchased a beautiful gold carpet for the living room and down the hall. I papered the kitchen and bathroom walls. I painted the other rooms, and it really began to shape up. The owner agreed to give us a percentage of the rent for two years, and that would go towards the down payment. The most beautiful thing about the house to me was the ceiling-to-floor window in the living room. When it snowed, it really looked like a picture postcard.

Does God Have Favorites?

Albert got a job with a relatively new company at the time called Digital Equipment Corp. We both decided that one of us needed to go and finish college. Since he had the potential to be the biggest earner, being male, and his field was booming, he decided to enroll in night school at Boston University. He challenged as many classes as he could. He was also credited with most of the courses from Golden Gate University. He won the university's highest academic honor, the Harold C. Case award. He was, and as far as we know, the only Metropolitan night school student to ever earn that award. We were all very proud of him. He went to school in the snow, rain, and sleet. Albert was very smart when it came to technology. He was truly blessed to have found a field that he loved so much. Computers were his hobby. He was always reading and staying ahead of his craft.

Chapter 24: Expanding Community Connections

I began meeting other Black women when Albert started working at Digital. My best friend was Dorothy. She was so down-to-earth and could make me laugh. Dorothy pulled no punches; she told you like it was. She was a registered nurse. We all got together and decided to form a club. We called it Umoja, which means unity in Swahili. I am amused at that, looking back, because there really wasn't any unity. It was a social climbing group of the Who's Who. I was voted Vice President. We really, now that I think about it, never had a goal or a plan. We just elected officers and met at different houses. My house was probably considered the worst of the group. One of the members' husbands was a former player for the original Patriots football team. She and her sister had that status. One member's husband was a veterinarian, and one of our members was an artist who finally got her studio in Boston. One member's husband was a lawyer with many connections in Washington, D.C. One member was a retired principal. They were all professionals or married to a professional. I was a housewife with no college degree. I don't know why I was elected Vice President. They also formed a men's club and asked Albert to join. He didn't, but they made him Treasurer anyway. That was déjà vu for me. We wanted a name on the books that carried weight. He was a graduate of Boston University with honors.

Social Climbers

I asked one of our members if she was going to the Ebony Fashion Show. I had never been, but I had heard so much about it that I wanted to go, but I didn't have anyone to go with me. She said, "Yes, my husband, children, and I will be going, but it's going to be a family affair." I wished her well. Sadly, I wasn't happy to hear that her husband divorced her and married a white woman. She ended up in Boston, homeless on the street. Thankfully, I understand one of her daughters got her off the streets. I hated to see her suffer two indignities.

One member of the club, I babysat her child. She gave a party and told me she would invite me, but she didn't mix business with pleasure. I told her no explanation was needed. I was going to be too busy anyway to attend. I know she had to fight with her kid to take him home; he never wanted to leave my house. I felt good about that. That was more important than going to a stuffy party with all the phony people. The funny thing about this person is that her family lived across the street from my brother in Chicago. However, I was not considered part of her social circle.

Party Crashers
Marie came to visit me because her mother lived in Connecticut. The men's club was giving a formal affair at this place on Route 9. The after-parties were hush-hush because they didn't want certain people to come. I told my friend about it, and she said, "Get dressed, we are going to crash this mother." Dorothy had told me where one of the parties was being held, and we went there. They almost choked when they saw us. She let us in and asked, "Would you like something to eat?"

My friend said, "No, we just ate."

The women were in one room, and the men were in the other. My friend immediately went where the men were and found a childhood friend from Louisiana. His wife was the one with the Art gallery. They were part of the "in" crowd, not only because she had a business, but they were truly Creole. He went nuts when he saw my friend, and the party was on. All the guys began to dance with us, and the woman came running. When we left, all the men were going to follow us, and we were going to go to another party. When the women heard this, they began to make ultimatums. The men told us not to worry, they would come. We left there and fell out laughing. We went home and relished their anger.

We lived across the street from a large Irish family. They had a little boy the same age as Kevin, also Harry. The mother and I became friends. I would go over to her house because she had to be home at lunchtime when her husband would come home to eat. She was really bored with this life, but she had a beautiful home. Her home was one of the custom-built ones. She was afraid to leave the house, and when she did, she had to call her husband to get permission. We did crafts and other things together, but mostly talked.

Part 12

The GM Years

Chapter 25: Assembly Lines & Union Tensions

I got a job at General Motors (GM) on the assembly line. Framingham was the last plant to hire women, and the men acted like complete fools. It became Peyton Place. Men chasing other men about their wives. Wives chasing men. The parking lot was full, especially during the holiday season. You could purchase leather coats, perfume, jewelry, you name it. I applied with some others who told me they were hiring. They wanted me to work in the office, but I wanted to work on the line. I could make more money, and I thought it was exciting. The men would put nasty pictures of women on the manifold. Our bathroom was in the boonies. It took forever to go there. I thought about GM and the bathroom when I saw the movie Hidden Figures. I always had an easy job compared to some other jobs. The shop was in two divisions. It was all one building, but the train tracks ran through the middle of it. If you worked on one side of the tracks, it was considered good. If you were put on the other side of the tracks, that was where the hardest jobs were. You had to work 90 days without being absent or late. After that, it was almost impossible to get rid of you.

When Papa Came to Visit

My father came to visit me. I was taking care of the child I mentioned earlier, and he took all his time with this child instead of his grandson. He let Kevin burn his fingers on the stove because he wasn't watching him. I had left for the store for only a minute and came back to burned fingers. The other child was sitting in my father's lap, and Kevin was sitting on the floor, crying, holding his hand. We took him home during the week of Easter break because I had the time off and Harry was out of school. My father lived with my sister, Marion, in Rockford, Illinois. My mother requested that if he outlived her, please let him stay with Marion. Unfortunately, he almost caused her a nervous breakdown. We left and were driving and talking, and I can't remember what was said before I said Papa, I am your daughter. He almost knocked me over when he said, "That's what they tell me."

I said, "Papa, how can you say that?"

"How does any man know?" he asked, like he genuinely wanted an answer.

I knew from then on that it was one of the reasons for his ignoring me. I asked my oldest sister, LaRaine, and she said he knows better. She called him and cussed him out. Anyway, we got him home, and while I was there, I went into the bathroom and felt this knot in my stomach. I thought it was maybe food, but it continued to stay there.

It's NOT Cancer
When we returned home, I went to Dr. Young. He said he would have to operate because an X-ray didn't show what it was, and there were no scanning machines at that time. The first thing on my mind was that it was cancer. I asked if I could wait another two weeks before I had it, because I would have completed my 90 days at that time. He said yes. I went back to work and waited until I had a week over 90 days before I told my boss I had to have an operation. He was furious and told me I should have known this before my 90 days, and I replied that I had only found out three days ago. He was so angry with me. I put the horn on the steering wheel. Some I made up, and others were already made up, depending on the model of the car.

Bumped by Ulterior Motives
There was a white guy who always came over to my station during his breaks and lunch. He would talk to my boss. He tried to bump me from my position, but you can't bump anyone at the same level. All jobs on the line were considered the same, no matter how some were obviously harder than others. I guess the Union put that clause in to keep people from continually bumping others from their positions. The only jobs that you could bump were the sub-assembly jobs. Sub-assembly jobs were jobs where you created special designs for the car. For example, if it was a station wagon, they would make the sides look like wood and put it on that

car. They didn't work that often because requests for special things on a car were not as frequent as the regular cars that came down the line.

I went out the next week to have my surgery. When he came into my room and told me he closed me up. I started to scream that I had inoperable cancer, and it was no use in taking it out. He calmed me down and said, "You have a dermoid tumor on your stomach muscle, and it was a keloid. The only thing we can do is leave it in because the cancer rate is very low for that type of tumor. Or we can remove the muscle, but that would give me a gaping hernia."

They didn't have lasers then. He explained that while doing some lifting, such as lifting something heavy or shoveling snow, I pulled a muscle, and when it healed, it created a keloid. I guess it was rare because when I would put this down on my medical chart, the doctors would say, "Oh, you have a dermoid tumor."

I would say, "No, it's a keloid."

Some doctors had to look it up, and then they knew what I was saying was true. I was out for two weeks, then I asked, "Can I go back to work?"

"I really don't want you to go back. I don't think women should stand and work on that hard concrete floor."

"I feel fine," disagreeing with him.

"Come back in a week. I'll release you then."

I came back, and he wrote me a back-to-work letter under the condition that I would be doing my same job or a similar related job. After visiting the medical department and presenting my release, which sent me back to my post, I found my apron and was informed that I no longer worked on that line. The supervisor would take me to the location where I had been assigned. I began to balk, and the supervisor said to go on so that I wouldn't be written up for insubordination. Of course, they put me on the other side of the tracks, and guess who was in my job? The man who came every day during his break.

I told them to get my union steward immediately. They said they would as soon as they showed me my job. They put me on the transmission. I had to torque the transmission. They showed me how many turns it takes to torque it. I did a few with them, looking at me. They left, and my union steward didn't show, so I began to burst all the seals on the transmission. I would ratchet it until I knew they were busted. A transmission can't be fixed. Once it's busted, it is trash. They came down because these seals kept coming down the line broken. They asked me to show them how I was torquing the transmission, and I did it just like they told me. They were scratching their heads, wondering why they were coming down broken. Dumb Dumbs. I cut my hand and had to be relieved. I went to the nurse, and she bandaged it and sent me back. I asked where my union steward was, whom I had asked for two hours before. They promised they would send him right away. He did by the time I got back to the transmissions. I told him I was released by my doctor, based on my return to my original job. I told him about the man who was there now and how he talked to the supervisor every chance he got because he wanted my job. I told him I would have my doctor rescind my release unless they brought me back on the other side of the tracks. I also said the supervisor was angry with me because I went out three weeks after getting in my 90 days. He insisted I knew before the 90 days. The union steward said he would take care of it. I finished that night shift. I was worn out from handling those bulky, heavy transmissions. I came in the next night, and before I got through the door, they told me to go to my old job. I thanked them. I kept that job until the changeover. I knew when I came back, they would put me across the tracks.

    When we came to Framingham, I met Rick and his wife. They lived in Boston, and we met them through some friends we helped out until they could find housing. I took to Rick right away. He became like a brother, and I loved Rick. His wife didn't care for me. Rick was from Cincinnati, and he and his mother knew my family that lived there. He loved my cooking, and we could talk all the time. He and his wife came to dinner, and she didn't say two words the whole evening. I tried to make small talk, but to no avail. I asked Rick if we had offended her, and he said no; she was just that way when she didn't know a person. I think she was jealous of our relationship. I was way too old and happily married for her to be jealous. His wife worked for Alma Lewis School in Roxbury. It was a well-known school of the arts. Sammy Davis Jr. and other entertainers backed it. They had so much talent in that school. His wife had the most beautiful voice I'd heard in a long time. We were invited to attend the Black Nativity. It was the most beautiful production I have ever seen. Kevin was only three years old, and he was mesmerized. He never took his eyes off the stage and was quiet the whole show. Rick's wife was very frustrated with Rick because he had finished at Howard University, but hadn't paid his fees, and they wouldn't release his diploma. He didn't and wouldn't work unless it was to his liking. He and his wife knew the only Black General Manager in GM. I guess she appealed to him, and he got Rick a job there. She was so happy because GM paid well, and their health plan was the best. She was pregnant and couldn't go to the doctor because she didn't have any money. They virtually lived off of her little salary. After the changeover, I couldn't believe Rick and I were on the same line right next to each other. Again, I got an easy job, and everybody accused me of sleeping with the general manager. I didn't even know him until he came down one night, and Rick introduced him to me. He did try to hit on me and visited me several times. I put the strip down the hood with pal nuts and Rick had a harder job putting the fiber glass under the hood. We would work ahead so we could play chess. They soon said we couldn't do that.

    All the Black men in GM treated me and the other Black woman well. They really looked out for and after us. They would come and talk to me every night. One of the men was a sweeper, and he looked like a Black Groucho Marks. He was so funny. He had a lot of kids and lived in Boston. He would entertain me with stories, and some nights we would all pile into a car and go to Boston to an all-night barbecue place. I would call Albert to see if he wanted anything. Sometimes he would and other times he wouldn't. He never gave a thought to my male friends. Albert did not lack self-esteem, and he never felt threatened. Another guy was Charlie. He was gay, but he would come in and call all the men sissies. He called me Tricksy. He would ask us what we wanted to eat and bring in Chicken, ribs, you name it. He would threaten the guys and tell them it was for me, not for them, but of course, we all ate. He came in later than we did on the line. He worked in the paint shop. He would warm up our food in the ovens in the paint shop.

Chapter 26: Expecting Geneá

    I began to have trouble with my birth control and was going to have it removed. I had to choose between having my tubes tied or having a baby. Albert said he would sign if I wanted to have my tubes tied. Imagine someone else having power over your body. My girlfriend Dottie said, "Cora, you should think about it. You've always wanted a girl."
    "Yes, that's true. But suppose I end up with My Three Sons?" I said jokingly, using the title from the then-well-known TV sitcom.
    "If you don't try, you are going to be sorry," she persuaded.
    Deep down, I knew she was right. There was no question that I wanted a daughter. So, I let her convince me to get pregnant. Albert had told me, "Whatever you want to do, you've got my support."
    I was told many different methods to use to have a girl. I tried them, and I guess it worked. I told my supervisor I was pregnant. He reminded me that I wouldn't have any special privileges because I was pregnant. They tried to show me by making me work overtime. Most of the time, they would poll the people to see who wanted to work overtime. This was bringing in the cars in the yard that needed repair. It was only twice that I worked overtime, and that was because they decided to run the line overtime. They always had volunteers to work the yard. If they told you that you had to work, then you had to work. They told me I had to work overtime, and several guys volunteered, and they said I had to. I suppose they were going to make an example of me. I really didn't feel like working. The guys told me what to do to get out of it. They said when they send you out to get a car, come into the building faster than usual and hit the pole. Of course, I got the first car with no brakes. I don't know how they expected me to stop with no brakes; they didn't give me any instructions. Well, all hell broke out, and they immediately got me out and escorted me to the nurses' station. I had to use the bathroom, and I wasn't

playing when I came out and told her I was spotting. She immediately sent me home. Well, I was never asked again. They basically left me alone after that.

    GM was fascinating in some ways. To follow pieces being put together and end up with a car was really clever. The line was designed with unbelievable precision. It never stopped unless something happened to make it stop. One night, one of the workers was so drunk he fell on the line. They dragged him off before he could do any damage. The workers would also become angry with their supervisors and put bottles in the doors, so when the car stopped, it would cling. You had to disassemble the entire door to determine the cause. They gave us pep talks about how we had to up our scores because if we didn't, they were going to close the plant. It didn't seem to matter, and I don't think they thought they meant it. Everybody knew not to buy a car made on Friday or Monday. We got paid weekly on Thursday, and half the plant didn't show up on those two days. They would get students from Framingham State, and of course, they didn't know what they were doing. The two problems I observed at that particular plant were supervisors who lacked job training in people skills. They were people who became supervisors based on seniority. They didn't seem to have any other skills. Consequently, there was always a problem with them and the workers. The workers could only vent through the union or take their anger out on the cars.

    As my pregnancy progressed, I soon had to go on maternity leave. I enjoyed being home and having a simpler lifestyle. Albert and I weren't passing each other like ships in the night. Charlie came to see me to bring me a present for the baby. He came and said, "Haven't you had that elephant yet?" Charlie could always make me laugh

    The closer I got to my due date, the more I had to go to the doctor almost every day. I was so large that he thought I might be having twins. He sent me for an X-ray. They saw only one baby. I asked the technician, "Can you tell if it's a boy or a girl?"

    He said, "Just hope it's normal."

    I almost flipped out. I went to see my doctor the next day, and I told him what he said, and he said he didn't see anything abnormal; it was just a large baby. I was so large that when I would sit down, my stomach would go past my knees. I always carried my babies all in my stomach. The doctor said he suggested I have a C-section because the baby was what they call a floater. Every day, she was in a different position, and if I went into labor as big as she was, either she or I might not make it. He scheduled the C-section. It was funny because as they were prepping me for surgery, my water broke. The doctor said I could try to have the baby normally, as it was in the birth position, or have a C-section. He suggested having the C-section, and since I was already prepped, I told him to go ahead.

Geneá was born at 8:30 am on March 26, 1974. She weighed 11 lbs. 3 and a half ounces. She was 22 inches long and beautiful. They put her in an incubator because she didn't come through the birth canal. She had a lot of mucus, and they needed to monitor her. She was the talk of the hospital until a boy was born two days later, weighing 12 lbs. I couldn't hold her for a day or two because of the anesthesia. I couldn't try breastfeeding her either because they didn't want her to get any of the medicine in her system. By the time they brought her to me to try and see if she would latch, she wanted no part of the breast. She was drinking more than four ounces per feeding.

I was so miserable because at the time they gave me that surgery, the bikini cut was not in existence. They cut me from top to bottom and closed all the air in the hospital inside me. The gas had me crying, and Albert had come but came empty-handed. All the other mothers had flowers and presents, and I had nothing but gas and misery. I called Aunt Clara to tell her I had a girl, and she noted in my voice that I was depressed. She sent me a beautiful bouquet, potted in a baby buggy, the next day. Albert then saw that, after seeing the flowers, he should have brought me something. He went down to the gift shop and brought me a beautiful bouquet.

They wouldn't let Kevin come to see me. He was considered underage. They encouraged me to walk to try to get the gas to move. It was very painful for me to walk. I felt my guts were going to fall out. But I did as much as I could. I would walk to the end of the unit, and Kevin could see me from the other side of the door.

My neighbor came one day with a beautiful pink dress for the baby. I was crying, and she asked what was wrong. I told her I was miserable with this gas. She asked what they were giving me. I said nothing but instructions to walk. She went to the nurses' station and requested some warm prune juice. Before she left, I began to blow out gas. I had to apologize to my roommate. She said it didn't bother her, and she would rather hear me fart than cry.

Does God Have Favorites?

I went home after four days, and when we got to the house, my neighbors had put up a sign and balloons, Welcome home, Mama and Geneá. I brought her home in the dress my neighbor had brought me. I had another outfit, but this one was cuter. I was so glad to be home. We had trouble with Kevin from the first day because he wanted to hold her, and I was concerned that he couldn't support her head, given that she was the size of a 3-month-old. Kevin would act up every time Harry could hold her, and he couldn't.

Looking back, I really didn't prepare Kevin for his sister. I regret not being more understanding of what he was going through. All of the attention was on Geneá, and suddenly, he was no longer the baby of the house, and Harry adored his little sister. Kevin began to act out. One night, I was awakened by the crying of the baby, and when I went to reach for her in the bassinet next to my bed, she wasn't there. I panicked and heard this thud and running. Kevin had picked her up out of the bassinet, put a bottle of milk on the stove, and when she started to cry and heard me coming, he put her on the clothes hamper and she rolled off. Of course I called the doctor and he asked us to examine her to see if there were any bumps and not to let her go to sleep for a while. She was fine, but I don't have to tell you what happened to Kevin. That was also the wrong response to his intentions. As parents, we make a lot of mistakes and, unfortunately, too often, we don't see them until it's too late. Albert's family sent her a lot of clothes, but they were all too small. They were sizes for a newborn. I donated them to Goodwill.

The Passing of Albert's Father
Albert was going on a trip to Los Angeles for Digital. He left for the airport when I got a call saying that his dad had passed away. I was so sorry, and I told them that Albert was on his way to California and I would have him get in contact with them as soon as he called. About an hour later, Albert came home. I asked him why he didn't go on the trip. He said he was, but the plane had been delayed 5 hours, and he didn't want to stay at the airport. I told him his father had passed, and he immediately called and told them his schedule, and he would come up as soon as his meetings were over.

The next night, I had a dream, it was more like a nightmare, it was so real. We were all in bed, and I awoke to the whirring sound. I got up, and there were these little people all over my living room. They were on the back of the sofa, but they didn't seem to see me. I opened the door to the garage, and there was an opening to the attic, which was also open. This bright, blinding light was coming down, and so were these little people. I ran back to my room, got the boys up, and put them in my bed. As I began to lock the door, I thought I didn't have Geneá. I opened the door, and in front of her room stood Mr. Brown, Albert's dad. I tried to get around him, and he stopped me and said, "I'm not going to let you have her."

I said, "Oh no."

Then we wrestled until I could get her and brought her into my room and locked the door. I later awoke, and my bed was completely destroyed where I had fought with him. I had to get up and change the sheets. I was afraid to open the door. The first thing I did was check on her and the boys. They were okay, and I changed my sheets, but I brought her into bed with me. It was the most vivid dream I have ever had. I don't consciously dream every night, and I have never had a nightmare except when I thought Harry's situation was a nightmare. It took me a long time to go into the hallway without a light on. I called my sister Marion and asked her what she thought of the dream. She said she believed that Mr. Brown came to either see her or take her. If he had taken her, it would've been crib death.

The last time I saw Mr. Brown was in December, and Geneá was born in March. He never saw her. At that time, she was the last grandchild on both sides of the family. Mr. Brown loved his children and grandchildren.

When she was 3 months old, I had her baptized at St. Bridget's. The priest wanted us to join, but we told them we were both divorced. That was the end of that. He kept calling Geneá, Genoa. We spell her name like the male spelling of Gene, with an accent mark over the "a" that makes it Geneá. Most people call her everything but Geneá. Most people spell it with a J. We had a big reception at the house, and she received many gift cards and money. I had to decide whether to return to GM or find other employment, as my maternity leave had come to an end. I chose not to go back to GM.

Chapter 27: Working for Digital

I applied to Digital Equipment Corp., where Albert was working, and was hired in the newspaper department as an editor. I found out about Ms. Lewis and her granddaughter and hired them to sit with Geneá. It was summertime, so I didn't have to worry about Kevin until the fall. Harry was out of school, and he kept him. Kevin wouldn't do anything for Harry. One day, they were riding their bikes on the street where the hospital was, and Harry told him to look out for the car, and he ran into a pole. He burst his forehead open. I came home and called his doctor, and he said to bring him in. He looked at his forehead and said he would need stitches and to take him to Framingham Union Hospital. Kevin had the sweetest doctor. He worked on Patrick Bouvier Kennedy and had a letter of appreciation from Jacqueline Kennedy framed in his office. During one of Kevin's visits, he kicked the doctor in his private area. He almost went to the floor.

"I'm so sorry my son kicked you. I don't know if you'll make it," I said apologetically.

"I'm going to make it," he said. "I don't know if you will make it."

When we got to the hospital, they began to ask Kevin questions. The questions were slanted toward child abuse. He wouldn't say anything and kept looking at me, which really made it look suspicious. At the time, child abuse was on the rise, and I guess they were only trying to see if this was the case. I informed them that at the time of the accident, I was at work, and I had witnesses who confirmed my presence at work at the time of the accident. His brother also testified that I was at work. They saw me getting upset and put Kevin on this board to stitch him. There was no place to numb the area, so they strapped him down because it was going to be painful. He was so strong that he broke free of the straps, and it took three people to hold him down. We took him home, and they advised me to put ice on it. He didn't like that, so I could only do it a little at a time. It wasn't two weeks that Kevin got angry with Harry and put his arms through the glass window. He had cuts all up and down his arm. Harry was so smart. He took towels, wrapped his arms, and went across the street to the neighbor, who was a nurse. She said he did the right thing. He came and called me at work. Again, I had to take off from work. I got home and called his doctor again, who said to take him to Framingham Union. I told him that if I took him there, they would surely arrest me for child abuse because they had questioned him about me causing the gash on his head. He said he would call the surgeon who did my surgery and see if he would take him in his office. He called back in a few minutes and told me to take him to Dr. Young.

    I was angry with Kevin this time because the first time he hurt himself, it was an accident; this time, it was him acting out. We went to Dr. Young's office, and he looked at his arms. He said he would have to shoot numbing fluid in every cut, and it would hurt. I told Kevin that he had better not cry, and his arms would be sore the next day. I couldn't believe he didn't cry because I was about to cry seeing him get that many stitches. His arms had 22 stitches between them. We took him home and again tried putting ice on them. The next morning, he got up, and before he could say anything, he said, "My arms don't hurt." I knew they did, but he was determined to make me wrong.

    I applied for and got another job in addition to the newspaper job. They wanted tour guides to run tours of the mill where Digital was housed. This mill was used in the Civil War and made blankets for the soldiers. It was vast in area and had really eerie doors and places we couldn't go in. They gave us maps and tours of the building. We would run tours two days a week. The other days I worked in my newspaper job. I really loved doing the tours. There was always a group of interesting people, and they asked all sorts of questions. Some of the floors in the mill were beautiful because of the oil from the wool. I later applied for a telephone position and was hired as the assistant telephone supervisor. I worked for a really wonderful but a little daffy lady. She wore beautiful jewelry and clothes. She married a very wealthy man, and they lived in a large house. She would tell me stories of what she would do when she went home. She didn't cook and wasn't domestic at all. She said she put on gloves to make her bed. I have no idea what that was for. She and I would go to seminars, and I would follow her in my car, and we would go through all of these beautiful neighborhoods on the way back. When we got back into the office, we had a wonderful time discussing these houses over lunch. I got this job because of my experience with the Telephone Company. I was assigned to visit the different groups in the mill and determine their needs in terms of phone usage and the number of people in each group.

    Digital was growing by leaps and bounds, and I was so busy that they hired another person to work with me. She was a little blond girl who made it plain I was not her boss, and we were equals. We weren't equals because I had more experience and seniority than she did. I let it go. She was supposed to take the orders and schedule my visits. Digital had its own telephone system. They didn't and weren't connected to the town's telephone company. We placed orders for repairs and installations with them, just as I had done with the Telephone Company in California. I walked so much in heels that I had a hard callus under the ball of my foot. It was so painful. It felt like a sharp pin sticking in my foot. I made an appointment with the podiatrist. He was a friend of the veterinarian in Framingham. He said he wanted to fracture my toe surgically. He said that my big toe was not taking the bulk of the weight that it is designed to do, and when it shifted to the next toe, it caused it to turn in and rub against the ball. He said he would fracture that toe to force the big toe to do what it was supposed to do. I made an appointment for the surgery. I was awake the whole time, and we talked about everything. Among the conversations was the bourgeois negros in Framingham. They had asked him to join this new club they were starting, but not tell his friend because they didn't want to embarrass him. He said, "Embarrass me how?"

    "We're going to go to places that cost more money than he has."

    "I didn't want to join. The idea of them excluding his friend for that purpose was an affront to him. They were so warped in their thinking. My friend has more money than I do," He continued. "My friend worked at the post office and was really savvy in dealing with money. In fact, he loaned me money before his business became lucrative."

    I told him about how they treated me, and he wasn't surprised. I was sitting up during the surgery, but he had me lie down because he didn't want me to see him fracture my toe. I was out for about two weeks. He suggested I wear a flat cushion shoe. It was very hard to find one that was acceptable for work. I finally found a pair, and it was better, but I later found out my big toe did not step up to the plate, and the next toe tried to take its place. All of my family had trouble with their feet because my father had the worst feet of anybody I knew. He would come home and work on his feet every night. He had bunions, corns, you name it. It seems the bones in his feet didn't develop as they should, and they didn't know about a podiatrist, even if they had, they wouldn't have been able to afford to go to one.

Manassas Class Reunion
In 1976, Manassas was having its class reunion. They asked me to please come, even though I didn't graduate with them. We still kept in touch, and since their class was the last to finish before they integrated Manassas, they were trying to get everybody who had attended to come back. I planned to go on vacation with my family. One day, I was looking through a magazine and found out that people were starting to hold family reunions. It seemed that a lot of Blacks had left the South in search of better jobs and education. Some families and friends stayed, and they began to know that coming together was fun and brought people in the family who didn't know each other. I found out that my father was in Memphis at a church conference, and my brother and sister-in-law were coming through Memphis to pick him up. I called my sister Marion and told her we were coming to Memphis, and why didn't she try to come? We could start a mini-reunion. We had a lot of family still living in Memphis, and with us coming and them, we had a wonderful family and high school reunion. I took Marian, my babysitter, with me to help me with Geneá. She had never been out of Framingham, and she was in heaven. She could really dance, and we were quite entertained.

We decided to keep the reunion going, and we would have it every other year, giving families a year to do something else. We decided to rotate the event and have different families host it. Marion said she wanted to host it in 1978. I was the secretary, and I took on the task of sending out information as well as collecting information. It was a task because my family was all over the United States. I worked tirelessly because, first, family always meant a lot to me, and secondly, I wanted my children to know their family.

Although we had accomplished a lot in Massachusetts, I never felt at home there and wanted to go back to California. Albert had obtained his degree; he was awarded Key Man Stock. We had another child, bought our first house, and Harry was truly happy because he played every sport known to man. He was a natural in all of them. He played hockey, soccer, and most of all Pop Warner football. He received the Most Valuable Player award one year. Harry likes to win and will push himself and anybody playing with him to the max. I still wanted and longed for California. Everybody in Framingham said they wanted me to go home because they were tired of me talking about it.

One day, I came home from work and all hell had broken loose. Harry told me my neighbor, who was my friend, had "hit Kevin."

"For what?" I demanded.

Harry explained they were all outside under the tree, and my neighbor's little boy was riding his bike. Kevin's bike was broken. Kevin was playing with his toy bear. Kevin asked the little boy to ride his bike, and he could play with his bear. It was agreed, but when the little boy wanted his bike back, Kevin wouldn't give it to him. He would run after Kevin on his bike, and Kevin would push him away. In doing this, he somehow scratched his face. The little boy went home crying, and the mother came out, yanked Kevin off the bike, and spanked him. She took her little boy inside and threw his bear in the street.

"She didn't spank him?" after listening to Harry.

"She did, but Kevin wasn't hurt," Harry said.

"That isn't the point," I said, agitated. I called her.

"Did you spank Kevin?"

"Yes! And I would do it again because Kevin is bad and spoiled," as she screamed on the phone.

"I can't and won't allow you to hit my child. I would never hit yours, and if you can't come to me to handle the punishment, I'll have to report you." I explained at the top of my voice.

"I will," she screamed and hung up the phone.

I was shaking, I was so angry and disappointed in someone that I considered a friend. If she had said she was sorry and done it without thinking, or anything other than "I will do it again," and then she did the ultimate, hanging up the phone on me. I cannot stand for someone to disrespect me. It says to me you have dismissed me.

The Hatfields and the McCoys Remix

I was livid when Albert came home. I told him what had happened. He didn't want to do anything. He didn't want to rock the boat. I told him I was going to take her to court if something couldn't be done about her threatening to hit my kid again. He called and got her husband on the phone. They agreed to meet and try to work something out, but I was not allowed to go. I said that wasn't fair because she would be there, but I wasn't allowed. Albert told me to calm down. He went over and met with the husband, and she took over the conversation. Nothing was settled except that they would not be able to play together. I didn't see how this was going to work with us being right across the street from each other. We had another incident where the little boy was not allowed to come to the house. It wasn't two days before he was at the door pleading for Kevin to come and play. They were children, and when adults get involved in children's play, it often ends up with the adults at odds. Since I wasn't heard and was shut out, I went and filed against her. She was served. She went to our other neighbor, all in a panic, asking what she should do. The neighbor suggested that she might want to apologize and promise not to hit Kevin again. She was not willing to back down. We went to court and the judge had me come and tell my side of the story. He had her come and tell her side of the story. He then had Harry come and tell what happened. The judge said he believed Harry, and he admonished her and asked her why she couldn't get along with her neighbor. He said he wanted her to apologize for her behavior, and we were to work things out. We were to come back to court on the day he set. She never complied, and I never spoke to her again. I decided not to go back to court and let it be. Of course, that broke the relationship Harry had with her son, and we became the Hatfields and the McCoys. Kevin and her little boy were to start school in the fall. She went up to the school and insisted that her little boy not be in the same class. They said they would not remove him from the class. They would get along. The problem I had was that the bus stopped in front of her house, and I didn't want Kevin alone. The bus agreed to come across from me and pick him up. The girls began to shout taunts at us and called us black bunnies or anything else negative. I told Albert we would either have to move somewhere else or go back to California. We tried to find another house, but the ones we found and could afford were not suitable for me. I told Albert I couldn't take it any longer, living with insults and not feeling free outside. We had a lady who was in the original club come by, and she heard and saw the insults. She said, "How long have you been living like this?" I told her too long, and what happened. Instead of her offering comfort, she said that this type of thing didn't happen in her neighborhood. That made me feel good. I'm being sarcastic. Albert finally knew that I was going to leave and go back to California with or without him. He received a transfer to Digital, but they didn't have any openings in my department. They offered to let me know when something came up. I really didn't care. I knew I would find something.

Cathy's Homework Assignments

We needed to sell our house, but we weren't getting bids for even near what it was worth. I felt this was again a color thing. The company offered to buy it so we could move. I was so happy to leave Massachusetts. Harry was unhappy because he had been accepted to the Catholic High School there, and he had friends and was happy living there. But we had an incident with a little white girl, named Cathy, who kept calling and claiming that she was trying to get homework assignments from Harry. The truth was, she really liked Harry. They even planned to go to the movies until her mother discovered that Harry was Black. After that, her mother called and said, "I do not want Harry to call my house anymore."

"I assure you, if you assure me that Cathy will not call my house," I countered.

Well, it was less than a week later when Cathy called my house again. "Does your mother know you're calling Harry?" I asked.

"Yes, my mother has given me permission to call and ask for the homework assignment," she lied.

Harry can't talk right now, but I'll let him know you called," I informed her. After she hung up the phone, I was so conflicted. Cathy was so innocent. But I felt that her mother needed to know, and I needed to be assured that Harry had not called her, not to mention the fact that it irritated me that Cathy's mother believed that her child was better than mine.

So I called and asked her, "Has Harry called your house?"

"No. Thank you for keeping him from calling my house," she said.

"I hate to tell you, but your daughter just called my house," I informed her.

"I am going to break her neck," she fumed as she hung up the phone.

I knew everybody wouldn't be happy, but as they say, when Mama's not happy, nobody is happy. We finally left. I really felt nostalgic about leaving the house and the struggle of getting it. It was our first, and although things turned out the way they did, we had some good times there. I did a final walk through the house and said goodbye to it. That was my only regret in leaving Framingham.

Chapter 28: Back to California

We went to San Jose to look for housing because Albert worked in Santa Clara. Santa Clara is next to San Jose. We stayed in a hotel and began to look for houses. My mother-in-law referred us to George. He sold her house on 16th Street, and she moved in with her oldest son. It was a Godsend finding George. He was married to a lady from Memphis. We knew each other's families. George was also a really good realtor. He began to show us houses, and we put Harry and Kevin in school near where we thought we would buy. I also got in touch with Earl in Oakland. He was quite a character, but I loved Earl. He was also a realtor. I asked Albert if he would mind commuting from the Bay Area, and he said no. He was in Sales, and he was given a company car to drive.

I looked in Oakland, and the only thing we could afford was a house way up in the hills. It had no view, just hundreds of trees. It was a great house, but in need of repair. We had a down payment and not a penny more. Someone had trashed the house. We would have had to put in new doors, carpet, paint, and repair the deck. I also didn't like the fact of driving that far into the hills without a view. So, we settled on looking for houses in San Jose. I later regretted giving up so easily on the bay. I did not like San Jose. The Black people reminded me too much of Massachusetts.

I think living in the hotel and driving the kids to school and picking them up was a chore; I just wanted to get settled. The baby and I would drop off the boys at school, and then we had nothing to do until we picked them up. It was also a time span between when I picked up Kevin and Harry. It wasn't long enough for us to go across town to the hotel and get back in time. It was a dilemma because it was too long to keep the children in the car until he got out. We would go to Albert's mother and brother's house to wait. That soon became awkward because one day I was watching TV, and I didn't notice the kids in the kitchen near the table where his mother and brother were eating. She asked me if they had eaten, and I said yes, and her response was to get out of here. I immediately heard this and told them to come and sit with me on the sofa. They were little kids and had a lot of energy. I left after that, even though we still had time until Harry got out of school. We went to the school, and I let them run around on the grass in front of the school until Harry got out.

    We found a house in the Berryessa area. I really liked it because it was built on the Spanish Casa. The family room was really small, but I didn't care. George directed me to a house near the kids' school because it had been on the market and the owners had bought another house, and they were eager to sell. The price was lower than the Berryessa house. I didn't like that house. Albert told me to stick with what I wanted. George and Sandra lived in the same model house across from the area where my house was. He took me to his house to show me how they had decorated. It was beautiful, but I still wanted the Berryessa house. George told me we probably could get into the house near their school in about two weeks. It would take a month or more to get Berryessa.

    At this point, I wanted to get settled. We didn't qualify because of the bills in Framingham. We had the down payment, but our credit wouldn't let us get a loan. The price of the house was $60,000. That is unbelievable now in 2025. George said he would buy the house for us and quit-claim deed it to us in 90 days. We were grateful to him for the offer. It was approximately two weeks later that we moved into 2308 Portal Way. Our furniture had arrived and was being stored. We got everything out of storage and began to set up housekeeping. I was working one day unpacking, and my next-door neighbor came over and introduced herself. Her name was Bonnie, and we hit it off right away. She would say, "Come on over and have a drink and be somebody." She was a schoolteacher. She had had a heart attack before we moved in, and her mother-in-law was there to help her. Bonnie came from Texas and worked her way through college. She worked with Connoley, who was the governor. She worked as a substitute, but not every day. She really had a bad heart. She told me all about San Jose. She said if you were not a professional, the Blacks didn't accept you. Here we go again. I felt like I had jumped from the skillet into the frying pan. Bonnie was not like that, and as long as I had her, I really didn't care.

My Journey Through Life, Love, and Tragedy

Across the street, on the corner, lived the Van Es family. They were retired missionaries. Everybody in the neighborhood respected them. They were the most loving people I had ever known. They opened their house to anyone who needed a place to stay. They were not preoccupied with material things. It seemed that whatever they wanted, someone would give them. They never asked. The only thing she showed interest in was a chest I brought home from Indonesia. She had a daughter who was married to a doctor. The doctor was really down-to-earth and never made you feel less than. The daughter was just the opposite. She was snooty and didn't like the relationship I had with her mother. They would gently prod you into going to church with them. I had gone to a Black church to meet some other friends, but I was ignored. The minister shook my hand on the way out and invited me back, but no one else said anything to me. Ms. Van Es invited me to come to their church. She asked if I sang. I said yes, and she said that I could sing in the choir without being a member. I went with her to choir rehearsal. They received me warmly. Again, I was the only little Black face there. This church's denomination was the Reformed Church in America. It was once known as the Dutch Reformed Church. They opened it up to everyone by dropping the Dutch in their name, but it was still predominantly Dutch. The church I attended was named Church of the Chimes. It worked out well for them because Peter was getting to where he couldn't see well at night. After I joined an all white church, some of the Blacks wanted to know why I wanted to be there instead of in a Black church. I learned a great deal about how they conducted their business and managed their church. I also learned that they had fired the minister before the one who was there at the time because he would not marry an interracial couple. I thought their values were in the right direction.

The Van Es's invited Albert, and I was shocked when he said yes. He went and, unbeknownst to me, filled out a card for a visit from the deacons of the church. That Tuesday, the doorbell rang, and there they stood. I was upset because the children kept the bathroom a mess, and inevitably, people want to use your facility sometime during their visit. I told Albert they were there and immediately began to clean the bathroom. After they left, I asked Albert what on earth was going on. Early in our relationship, Albert told me he was never going to church because he had a bad experience when he was young. I told him he didn't ever have to go as long as he didn't try to stop me from going. So, you can imagine the surprise. He shared, "I can't explain what happened. When I went there, something overcame me, and I wanted to learn about the church." Albert ended up joining before I did. Harry never went to the church, but Kevin and Geneá went with us. Kevin had a good time because he had friends, and we later got a youth minister, who said that the group was tough to handle. I think he was new and young, but those kids were a handful. Geneá never took to the church, and she didn't want to go.

    Kevin was having trouble at school. I never knew how children could tell the difference in each other. He was being called names, and he wasn't sophisticated enough to fight back with words, so he lashed out with his fist. They never investigated why he was fighting; they just wanted to punish him. So, he was always the one in trouble. Harry was having a great time. He has always been outgoing, and people take to him. When he got into the 11th grade he started dating a freshman. They were so in love that he said they were going to get married. I just laughed. Geneá was friends with Bonnie's little boy. We have a picture of them kissing in front of the house.

    One of my friends from Framingham wanted to come and visit me. I was so happy. She was a down-to-earth, no-nonsense person. She was grateful that I helped her get a job at Digital. She was older than I, and she didn't think she had a chance of being hired. I constantly checked the openings, and I told her of three she should apply for. She got the one she wanted and stayed until she retired. She purchased a home there and had done very well for herself. I periodically call her and see who and what is going on. My friend Dottie passed away. Her children all did well for themselves. I was happy for her because she and her husband sold their summer home to get them through school. Some of the Blacks started a church. They had problems renting a small church that was not in use. They finally secured it. When she told me that they had built a lovely structure, I was happy for them. Anyway, she came, and we planned to visit Aunt Clara the next day and San Francisco the following day. I introduced her to Bonnie. We wanted her to go with us, but she said she would go the following day. She and her family had just returned from a trip to her home in Texas, and she said she was going to get her son and Harry to wash and clean the car. She had clothes that needed to be washed, and she needed to relax. We left for Aunt Clara's, and when we got in the door, Aunt Clara said, "Call Harry right away."

My Journey Through Life, Love, and Tragedy

When I called him, I couldn't describe how I felt after I heard him say, "Bonnie had a heart attack. She fell on the floor, clutching her heart, and said, 'Oh no.' They took her in an ambulance."

I was trying not to ruin my friend's visit, but I was devastated. Bonnie was such a ray of sunshine for me after spending five years with people who were haters. She was also the only person I knew besides George and Sandra. We came home, and it turned out that Bonnie had died when they took her to the hospital. Everybody was sad. We went to San Francisco the next day, and my friend from Framingham, knowing I wanted to help Bonnie's family, cut her visit short and left the next day. I went over to see what I could do. They said they were not going to have a funeral but a burial service just for family. I felt alone and crushed. Now it seemed that I would not be able to say goodbye to her. I wanted closure, and I never got it. My goodbye was waving to her in her driveway. I did take a ham over for her family. Her mother and sister came from Texas. Soon after her husband got married, he never introduced his new wife to anyone. They moved, I found out later, to Idaho. Bonnie was gone, and so were her memories. I was so devastated. "Why don't you go to the HOA meeting at the clubhouse. Maybe you will meet some other people," Albert suggested.

I attended the meeting and picked Melissa out of the crowd. For one thing, she was the only other Black woman there. Melissa ignored me. She and I laugh about it today. She confessed that she didn't know why she acted that way. We became friends, but Melissa had so many friends and family that I was not as special to her as I had been to Bonnie. She filled some of the void by introducing me to Jannell, another lady who lived in the track. Jannell and Donnell, her husband, were and are good people who helped everybody. Melissa was the oldest in her family. She had an older sister who was handicapped, so Melissa was always in charge. Some of her family said she was too bossy. Melissa didn't care and continued doing what she knew best, giving orders.

My dad passed away in March 1978 from prostate cancer. He had such a good time at the first family reunion that he made me promise to keep it going. Marion had services for him in Rockford and then in Memphis. Our cousin Howard appeared out of nowhere, and Marion was so happy to see him and that he had come. It seemed he had just left his job, got into his car, and came to Rockford. He was living in Baltimore, Maryland, at the time. After the service in Rockford, he went back to

Does God Have Favorites?

Baltimore, and we all went to Memphis. We all stayed at Aunt Katie's house. We had our dad's funeral at night, and he was to be buried the next day. We were all talking about old times when Aunt Katie teased, "I couldn't get loose at the funeral, but I'm gonna fall over the grave tomorrow."

Nick joked, "I hope you fall face-first so you can claw your way to hell, 'cause it will be that time before I try to get you out."

We all howled. Aunt Katie was known for her antics at the funerals. When my grandfather died, she acted up so that my Aunt Floyd kept punching her, telling her not to upset Mama in the country. She had to be carried out, feet first, at my mother's funeral. She was a character, but one that made me laugh.

In 1978, it was time for our second reunion. We all went to Rockford, Illinois. Marion was the host and had booked us at a fancy resort located right outside Rockford. I was glad that I could keep my promise to Papa to have the reunion no matter what happened. He had such a good time at the first one. Marion had made so much food. We began with a poolside picnic. The next day was the banquet. It began to rain in the morning, and by evening, when we checked into the resort, it was unbelievable. It rained so hard that there were leaks in some of the rooms, and people had to be relocated. That didn't daunt our spirit. This was one of the largest reunions. I think the word had gotten out how much fun the first one was. Most of our family also lived in Memphis, Illinois, Michigan, and Ohio. We had a wonderful time. When Aunt Katie came out dancing, Lester, my brother, had to rein her in. Aunt Katie was a character, and I truly loved her spirit, although some of her sisters didn't like some of her decisions and business dealings. She asked us to help her to her room after this dance. She confessed that she had done a little too much. She was the life of the party. The next day, it rained so hard that some of the bridges were washed out, and we had to be rerouted. We decided to go back to Memphis for the 1980 reunion. Lester had also suggested that we change the dates around the 4th of July to either before or after. He stated that the highways were really crowded and treacherous. We decided we would always have it after the Fourth of July. We also decided to start a treasury because it was too costly for the host or hostess to fund the reunion. We went home with Marion and left the next day for California.

My Journey Through Life, Love, and Tragedy

Digital offered me a job, but to this day, I haven't understood. I really can't tell you what I was doing. I was unhappy there, and I wanted to be considered for a program that would train me for a supervisor position. They never put me in for it. I began to look for a job elsewhere. I applied and got a job at Syntex Corporation, a pharmaceutical company. I worked in the Bio Statistics department. It was a wonderful job and great people. We would go to the park and have lunch on fine China and crystal glasses. Our boss treated us all to an overnight retreat on the beach and said it was a working weekend. We had a woman in the group who fished for abalone. She would bring it to work, and we would go to another lady in the group house and have lavish lunches. The company was the greatest. They would have picnics, and the bosses and doctors would serve us. Syntex was known for the first birth control pill. They tried other products, but none were as successful as Norinyl until they developed Naprosyn. It was a revolutionary drug. That was party time. After a drug is on the market for a certain number of years, it loses its patent, and Naprosyn became Aleve.

Albert was doing well at Digital and received awards for the business he brought in. He was the leading salesman. He discovered through The New York Times that the University of Hawaii had a United Nations contract to work in Indonesia. He applied and got the job. He told me, "I want to go to Indonesia. What do you think?"

"I want to go too," I agreed.

We began to look and see where Indonesia really was on the map. We had a problem in that Harry was going into the 12th grade, and we didn't, and he didn't want to go. Harry doesn't like change. George and Sandra were renting a house that cost them an arm and a leg. I spoke with Sandra and asked if she and George would be willing to rent from us, and we would offer them a significant discount if they allowed Harry to keep his room and stay with them. They agreed, and that was one thing settled. Another problem we had was getting our money to Indonesia. We were paid in American currency, and the American banks did not make those transactions. We found a company that was supposed to pay our bills, give Harry his allowance, and send the rest to us. They charged us a huge fee. The other problem was finding summer clothes. The climate in Indonesia is hot. Here in America, clothing stores had put out fall and winter clothes, and all the sales for spring and summer were gone. With some of the clothes we had and the few we found, we had enough. Then I wondered *what was I going to do with my hair?* I used a straightener in my hair, and I knew they didn't sell those kinds of products there. I had my friend send me the kit, and I had to keep it in the refrigerator to maintain the integrity of the ingredient that straightens the hair. One of the things I didn't have to worry about was sanitary pads. Their pads were so thin and small, I would not even attempt to use them. I had a hysterectomy right before we went to Indonesia. I was thrilled to undergo this surgery. I had soiled every seat I sat on. We had beautiful blue chairs at Syntex, but mine were black and stained. I could never wear white. When I went to see the surgeon, she asked why I was suffering like this. I had my tubes tied, and I couldn't have any more children. I would hemorrhage every month and had no energy. My doctor teased, "I don't know how you're walking losing that much blood every month. Let's schedule you for surgery."

Curious, Albert asked, "Will you start getting hair on your face?"

I told the doctor, and she made an appointment for him.

Because anatomy was not discussed in school or at home, she informed him, "that was normal for our age group." He felt better when she took him to school.

There was a couple that worked at Syntex who went to Indonesia for their honeymoon. When she found out we were going there, she introduced us to a lady who taught Bahasa Indonesia. I was so happy she did because she taught us enough to get along and know some of the basics. She also provided us with the names and numbers of Indonesians to contact, which could help us with translation. I didn't know what to pack. I didn't know if I had to bring furniture or what. We decided to take the essentials, and if we needed anything else, we would have someone send it to us. We finally had enough. I didn't know how easy it was to have something made in Indonesia. We got our passports and boarded the plane. We stopped in Hawaii, and Albert went to the University to get all of his paperwork signed and instructions. We really didn't see much of Honolulu. Albert seemed afraid for some reason to go out and sightsee.

Our next stop was Jakarta. This was one of the longest flights of many more I would have during our travels. I guess it seemed that way because it wasn't broken up like our flights from Vietnam.

Part 13

Jakarta, Indonesia

Chapter 29: Bustling Streets & Bamboo Headboards

We arrived in Indonesia in late August 1979, to the same hustle and bustle as Saigon: motor bikes, cars, throngs of people. I was thrilled. We stayed in one of Jakarta's most beautiful and prestigious hotels, named Hotel Borobudur. It was very exotic. The headboards were made of bamboo arranged in a very unusual pattern. It was in the middle of downtown. Albert went and reported to the Department of Finance. We started looking for housing. The United Nations doesn't provide housing for its employees, unlike the other expats working there. The oil companies had their compound. The Ford people had their compound, which was where President Obama's mother stayed when she was in Jakarta. The American Embassy workers had their compound. We were getting discouraged because we didn't have anyone or directions on where to look. One day, I went shopping and met a lady who became my friend. Her name was Carol. She was a lifesaver. Her husband was the head of IBM, and they provided them with all kinds of resources. They had someone to find their house, the best furniture makers, and all types of services for them. In talking and getting to know each other, I mentioned we were having difficulty finding housing. She said she would have her guy to help us. She said she wanted me to meet her boys. She was previously married to a Jamaican, and she wanted her boys to know their people. Carol and her husband, Myron, were of Polish descent. We exchanged numbers, and two days later, we went to look at a house on MPR 9 in Cilandak. It was beautiful with a step-down living room and luscious carpet. The master bath had an opening in the ceiling and an orchid wall. Two other bedrooms, a dining room, a swimming pool, and the kitchen were outside. In Indonesia, when you rent, you pay the whole year's rent when you move in. We paid the rent, but somehow, after paying for the hotel, food, and other amenities, we were broke, and we weren't due to receive another draw until after December. I never knew about the financial part of the contract, but I knew I didn't have any money for Christmas or anything else. We went to the church in hopes that they would let us have enough to tide us over until our next draw. Someone in the church informed the Embassy, and they sent a telegram to the University stating that they could not and would not have an American on contract with no money. They would send us a draw, and they didn't care how they worked it out. We got the money in two days.

When we moved into the house, we didn't have any servants. The room where Geneá slept had not been sprayed, and she was literally covered in mosquito bites from head to toe. I was so afraid because I didn't know what to do. When we arrived, the American Women's Association gave us a book with great information. We looked in the book for a hospital and took her there. They were more curious about us than about her bites. They gave us some medicine to put on the bites. It looked like Calamine lotion, and fortunately, she didn't contract malaria or any other illness from the bites. The landlord sprayed the room, and there were no more bites.

The next day, we went to register the children in school. Geneá started Kindergarten, and Kevin started the fourth grade. Geneá's teacher was Keith Clemson. Because of the name, you would think the teacher was a man, but she was a woman. She was so friendly and easy to know. The second day, I asked if she knew of anyone looking for a job. We didn't have any servants. The next day, she told me about a man who had worked for her, named Suhardi, but he was a cook and was accustomed to a household that hosted parties and other forms of entertainment. She referred him to another person who entertained often. The man she referred him to went away on a trip and was robbed while he was away. When he returned home, they questioned Suhardi and the guard (jaga). The guard lied about Suhardi and claimed he had done it. They took Suhardi's *Kartu Penduduk* (residence/ID card), and without it, he couldn't work. She said if we were willing to hire him, she would vouch for him until he could get it back. She said he was a cook by trade but worked in all capacities as a servant. She really liked him and thought the best of him. She said she was sorry she couldn't have kept him.

My Journey Through Life, Love, and Tragedy

     We interviewed Suhardi and immediately liked him. He came to work for us the next day. Through Safai, a servant who worked for Ms. Clemeson, Suhardi explained that he had to have every Tuesday off to go to the police station. We said that was alright with us. Safai also asked if we needed other servants. We said yes, we needed a baba cuci (someone to do laundry) and a jaga (guard). He said his brother and sister were looking for a job. We asked them to come over for an interview. He brought them two days later. They were a married couple. He was supposed to be the Jaga, and she the Baba Cuci. Her Name was Kartini, and she had a little girl named Uni. I don't remember her husband's name, but he didn't work out. He would argue with her, and one day, he hit her. We told him he had to go, but we wanted her to stay. She was torn because women were expected to obey their husbands. She stayed. I later found out that her husband was Safai's brother and she was his sister-in-law. In Indonesia, there is no such thing as in-laws. Safai told her and gave her permission to stay. Her husband would show up when she got paid and take most of her money. I don't know what happened to their relationship, but we didn't see him anymore, and Kartina, I think, began to see someone else. She was so beautiful and was named after one of their folklore queens. Life settled into a routine: the children were in school, Albert was working, and I attended the American and Canadian Women's meetings. I also took up the art of Batik. The children were in the children's sunshine choir. They performed at the AWA meetings. Our meetings were held at the Hilton Hotel. I also learned to quilt, make vanilla, and maple syrup. I joined the choir at St. Canisius Catholic Church. Carol and I always went shopping. I was also meeting some of the wives of the men who worked with Albert. I finally got in touch with Henny. She was a contact from our Bahasa tutor. She was also invaluable because she was an English teacher. I began to learn more Bahasa and was more comfortable bargaining. In fact, I became very good at it. They really got over on me at first, even though it was in the AWA book; you really had to work at it. Bargaining is not part of our culture. Whatever the price of the article, that is what we paid.
     Our first year was full of activities, meeting people, and shopping. Our first Christmas was spent partly with some other Black people we met. One of the couples was truly genuine and nice to be with, but they knew another couple who we were to have dinner at their house. I was informed that they were having marital problems. I could see why,

because the husband was too into himself. He strutted around like a peacock, and at dinner I asked him what he did for the embassy, and his answer was "I work there." Everybody at the table made me feel I had asked something that was totally out of place, including my husband. To this day, I haven't seen anything inappropriate about that question because everybody asked each other what their job was and the reason they were in Indonesia. Even if he was an undercover personnel, all he had to say was that he was on a government contract or he worked in the office of whoever. We had promised Carol that we would come to her house afterward, and I immediately wanted to leave. I only accepted the invitation because I thought these were Black people like me, but I was mistaken. They commented that, "You would rather spend Christmas with a white family than with us."

"It is not a matter of color to me; it was a matter of being accepted and comfortable in my surroundings," I rebuffed.

Also, we had two children who had no one there to play with. This was Christmas, a time that I always enjoyed and loved, and I didn't want to spend it uptight and miserable. We left and never saw the couple that we had dinner with at their house. We continued our friendship with the couple we had met before, and we maintained contact after all of us returned to the United States. She started a successful business and adopted a daughter. I regret having lost contact with her over the years.

It was nearing the end of the school year, and Harry was graduating from High School. The children and I went back for his graduation and to attend our family reunion. Albert said they were at a crucial point in his job, and he would stay and plan to go next year. Harry not only graduated, but he graduated with a full scholarship in Track. His record stood unbeaten for years. He chose San Jose State because that was the school his dad attended. We did have to provide housing, books, and other essentials. Albert had promised him that if he graduated and got into college, he would buy him a car. We didn't have the money to buy a car, and Albert was very upset because, as I said, he always did what he said he would do. I think Harry was disappointed, too, but he never said anything or showed it. He graduated, and his paternal grandmother came from Detroit. My sister was upset with me for letting Harry have a relationship with her. I never believed in involving my children in adult relationships. I felt she was his grandmother, and I wanted him to have a relationship with her. She brought him a beautiful travel bag. We left for the reunion two days later. George said I could take his car, but when he brought it to me, it was actually his wife Sandra's car. I felt bad for her because she was left with a stick-shift Mazda. George assured me she didn't mind. Knowing Sandra as I do now, even if she did mind, she would not express it. She is such a good friend and Christian. Harry did a lot of the driving, and we arrived in Memphis in one piece. I had some leather fans made with Shannon Rogers' Reunion on them. Everybody loved them. We had a great time as usual. Albert was to send me some money to have on the way back. The day before Sunday, I suggested to my Aunt Katie that we have dinner at her house. She said, "I save my Sundays for my male friend."

I said, "Okay," and on Sunday we all went to church.

My niece's mother invited us to her house for dinner. She said, "Cora, you know you are just like my child anyway."

After dinner, we kept going to Western Union for the money, and it didn't come. We had checked out of the hotel on Saturday, and now I was trying to save the money I had left. Aunt Katie was aware that I was waiting for the money. We asked if we could stay the night with her until Monday, in hopes that we would get the money. I had some money, but I didn't think I had enough to make it all the way back to California. We got into an argument.

"You didn't sit with me in church," she ranted. "And I made all of this food, and then you went to Vernita's house," she raged on.

"Aunt Katie, you told me you saved Sundays for your male friend," I countered.

"I didn't tell you that!" she argued.

One word led to another, and Harry said, "Come on, Mama, let's go back to the hotel." We went back and checked into the hotel. I called Marion because we were going to her house on the way back. She told me to come on Monday, whether the money came or not. I said we would. We found out that the money was not wired but sent through the bank and then mailed to Aunt Katie's house. I called her the next morning to see if her mail had run, and she said, "Yes, the check is here. I opened it to make sure that it really was the check." Right!!! The check was supposed to be in the amount of a thousand dollars, but I got nine hundred and some dollars because the bank had taken out fees. We got the check and headed to Marion's. This was becoming the second trip from hell. At that time, banks were not national. All banks were local to their specific area and didn't have relationships with out-of-state banks. Marion carried me to her bank to cash the check, and it seemed she had to promise to give up her firstborn for them to do it. They finally cashed the check. I went shopping for us to continue our journey home. We were to go through Los Angeles to see LaRaine and the children, and to visit Disneyland. Marion thought we should stay in a hotel rather than with LaRaine. I failed to ask her why. I think LaRaine had said something to Marion about me, and whatever it was, Marion thought it best to stay in a hotel. I didn't listen to her as I should have. I thought I could save money, and we needed to wash some clothes. We were going to leave Los Angeles and go to UC Santa Barbara. Harry had also been offered a scholarship there. We met Melissa and her family in Los Angeles, and we all went to Disneyland. The next day, we went to Knott's Berry Farm. Melissa asked if she could borrow some money until we got home to San Jose. She said she would come by LaRaine's and pick it up. I let LaRaine know that I needed to go to the bank to cash one of the traveler's checks. Melissa was to come later to pick it up. LaRaine told me to go to her bank because they knew her there in case I had a problem cashing the check. She also said we should take it easy and not do anything that day but relax. I told her I had planned to do that because I had a lot of clothes to wash. Everybody was busy doing something. Kevin was watching TV. Geneá was playing with a doll LaRaine had given her, and Harry was helping me with the clothes. Art was getting ready to go to his job at Disneyland, and LaRaine had put his food on the table to eat. The doorbell rang, and it was Melissa and her family. I invited her in, and they all sat on the sofa. LaRaine immediately asked if she could talk to me. We went out to the back, and she lit into me, "I told you we were not going to do anything today, and you have these people to come over here, and I don't have anything to offer them."

"What are you talking about? I told you Melissa was coming to get the money I was loaning her. You knew that when I asked you about cashing the traveler's check."

She acted as if I didn't say anything and just went off. I left her and went to Melissa and gave her the money. LaRaine came in and apologized that she didn't have any lunch to offer them. All of them said together, "We didn't come to eat, we just got through eating lunch. We've got to go. Are you going to be alright? If you need to, you're welcome to come with us to my cousin's house," she said, expressing concern.

"Thank you, but I want to finish washing," I reassured her.

When they left, LaRaine insisted, "You embarrassed me by having Melissa and her family come to my house."

" LaRaine, I told you why I wanted to go to the bank. And I told you Melissa was coming by to pick up the money. Did you want her to come and blow the horn, and I run out and give it to her?"

She didn't hear anything I said, and I just lost it. Again, Harry said, "Come on, Mama, let's go."

We were throwing clothes, both dry and wet, into bags and loading them into the car. She was trying to console Geneá because she began to cry from all the ruckus. We left, and I didn't look back or say anything else to her. I was afraid I was going to say or do something I would later regret. We found a motel in Santa Barbara because we were to meet the track coach the next day. I was disgusted and tired of being put into situations I didn't cause. I was tempted to cancel the appointment and let Harry come back later without us. We were unable to get in touch with the coach, so we had to proceed. I was so tired, angry, and disgusted. From Aunt Katie's attitude, not receiving the money as I should, and not heeding Marion's warning, I was getting depressed. I just wanted to go back to San Jose and then go back to Indonesia.

We got up the next morning and met the coach. He began to tell Harry about the program they had at UC and was trying to show us around the campus. Geneá, for some reason, began to act up, and there was nothing I could do to calm her down. She wouldn't let us talk, walk, or see any of the campus. The coach had planned lunch for us, but she cried and fell out and couldn't be consoled. It was so bad that even the coach commented that we needed to take her in hand. I don't know why she decided to act that way. Geneá was a happy-go-lucky kid. I later tried to analyze it. I think she became overwhelmed by all the travel, living in different hotels, the arguments I was having, and riding long distances. After leaving LaRaine's, this was her way of coping. Harry was disappointed that he didn't get a chance to really evaluate the school. We finally got back to San Jose. Some of the clothes had to be rewashed. We began to pack to leave. Harry hadn't moved into the dorm before we left. So, we left him still at home with Sandra and George. He later moved, and we had to send money to the school for him.

I can hardly begin to tell you how happy I was to return to the noise, hustle, and bustle of Jakarta. It was loud and dirty, but you also had the opportunity to get away from it all. Having servants was one of the amenities that took away a lot of the pettiness of life. I could go to the American Women's Club, and they had rooms just for meditation. I could also stay in the house and read or write, without worrying about the children, cooking, or laundry.

We returned to Indonesia, and we had moved to another house. It was way away from where we used to live. There were no other expats near us, and we lived next to a large compound. Everybody who came to visit us always questioned whether we were afraid of living so far out. I told them no. I was always comfortable around most Indonesians. We had a real good time there. We even celebrated one of our anniversaries.

I had met some women at the UN meeting. One was an American Filipino, and the other was from Ethiopia. We all became fast friends, and when my son and stepdaughter came over for the holidays, their children and my children partied all the time. The driver was making good money, but he asked, "When I sleep?"

He had an accident on himself and all the other servants laughed at him. He wanted our Baba Cuci to wash his pants. She refused. I know he was happy when they left. The American Embassy would bring over all of the Embassy workers children that was not living over there. They would have lunch and parties for them. They had said at first that Harry couldn't come because he was not Albert's biological child. You know, I went crazy. We had to get people from everywhere to write and tell them that although Harry was not legally Albert's child, Albert had raised him, and he was more a part of our household than his daughter. They relented because no one was going to come if Harry couldn't come. Suhardi was so impressed with Harry. Harry took a sickle and was cutting the grass. He also went for a run and got lost. He rode the city bus with his head out of the top of the bus. After they left, I continued to take batik. That was, and still is, a genuine interest of mine. We had so much fun in that class and with the teacher who taught it. I vividly remember the fight between Larry Holmes and Muhammad Ali. The Indonesian government, not legally but in jest, declared a national holiday. The whole neighborhood was looking through my window. I told Suhardi to let them in and give them something to drink. They were so thankful that I think they would have protected us from anything or anybody. It was around this time that rumors began to circulate about Sandra and Albert. He told me she was helping him get into an Indonesian company, and they could make a lot of money. My Indonesian friend began to ask me what was going on with them. I told them the same thing, so they didn't say anything else out of respect for me. I did ask him what their business was, and he gave me the same version I had just said, and not being a suspicious wife, I didn't think anymore about it. I continued to get accustomed to Indonesia. I bought tons of puppets. There was an American lady who helped this village. They would bring their puppets to her house, and we would shop, have tea, and chat. Puppets are a huge part of Indonesian culture. They were first known for their shadow puppets. They are called *Wayang kulit*. *Wayang* means puppet, and *kulit* means leather. Later, they created *Wayang golek*, with *golek* meaning wooden doll." The wood puppets were the ones I bought. The shadow puppets could not be displayed. Albert was later given a whole company of shadow puppets that were used in a show. Indonesian folklore fascinated me. They are beautiful people. They are warm, kind-hearted, and will give you almost anything you admire. I met Muki Reksoprojo and his wife. Muki was a doctor. He had come from humble beginnings, and the government had paid for him to attend school. His wife, Purti, was beautiful. His first wife died, leaving two boys, and he and Purti had two girls. They built a beautiful house in an up-and-coming area. Purti belonged to an Indonesian English club. She and I said we were sisters because we shared the same birthday.

    There was an organization called WIC. It was the Women's International Club. Every year, all the embassies would have booths and sell goods to the Indonesian women. It was said that they saved all year for this event. Everything sold had to be made in your country. Of course, we had fewer and fewer goods from America. The biggest seller was Ecco ware. It also seemed that whatever Americans sold, they wanted it. America has always been a place where everybody is rich. When tukangs (craftsmen) would come to the house to sell their wares, I would have Suhardi tell them I didn't have any money. He would never say that. He would say, "She no like." That was not true. To them, there was no such thing as an American not having money. Even among other cultures like my friend from Ethiopia thought all American's had money and to live and travel abroad of course you had money. Everything is relative.

    They have a somewhat class system in Indonesia, not as bad as India but they remained separate. I began taking Batik classes. Carol was also and this was quite an experience. It was also so much fun. It kept me busy. Albert was spending more and more time with Sandra. Our sex life began to suffer, too. Dumb me still wasn't thinking of him cheating on me.

Does God Have Favorites?

We gave an anniversary party, and Suhardi knew of a person who made centerpieces; they made us a quite elaborate one. All of the people I knew came, and so did Sandra. My friend, Inka, was quite surprised. We didn't have air conditioning in the main rooms, only in the bedrooms, and one of our guests, who was pregnant, was overcome with heat. She had to leave, and I felt really sorry for her. Carol and my Ethiopian friend kept going into the bedroom to get relief from the heat. It was a success despite the heat and Sandra. We were nearing Christmas again, and Harry and Angela were coming over. Carol and Myron came for dinner, and we had fun as usual. Carol was great to be around. Her attitude was always light and fun-seeking. The children had fun, and it was a lovely Christmas. It was again time to go home for the summer. Albert had finished his contract with the Indonesian Department of Finance, so we thought we were going home for good. Albert was approached and offered a job in the USAID department. He didn't know if he wanted to accept it or not. We paid our servants severance pay because we weren't sure if we would be returning. Suhardi was exceptionally sad. Albert had helped him get his ID card back, and he was so grateful. We left and brought some of our artifacts home.

    The following year, we returned home, and Albert bought Harry a car. We were home about a week, and Albert said that he and Harry were going to look at cars. Well, they not only looked at cars but traded our car in on a TR7. Harry always wanted a sports car, and I once had a TR3. Albert was offered a contract with USAID before leaving, and he didn't decide until we returned home. They came back with some lucrative offers and perks he couldn't resist. So he signed to go back, and that meant I had to stay and get things straightened out before returning. I got Geneá's hair braided so it would be easy to manage. The kids didn't want to go back with their dad. He was always harsh with them, and it took me to soften him toward them. But they had to go to school, and I didn't want them coming in late. The car presented me with a problem. How was I supposed to get around with no car and no bus system to speak of in San Jose? On top of that, Harry blew the engine right after Albert and the children left. That left us both with no car. It would cost $2,000 to fix it, which was almost what we owed on it. Albert was getting his severance from the UN, and it was $2,000. He said to have it fixed, and when the money comes in, to pay for it. We still had a problem with no car. One day, Harry came home and said that Marshall, an old friend, had been looking for me. He wanted me to get in contact with him, and I did. Marshall always kept two cars. My prayers had been answered. He brought me one of his cars to use. It was a hooptie, but it ran, and that was all I needed. Harry was getting rides with his friends. I had to go to the bank, and I finally got my friend to handle my money and send me the money after the bills were paid. I had to rent the house out, and Harry was supposed to manage it. I ran around trying to get products that we needed, and I finally got everything done. I paid for Harry's car, so he was back in business again. His dad told him it was his responsibility from then on to learn how to fix his car. He also warned him about racing his cousin, which led to the first engine failure. It worked because Harry became a quasi-mechanic, and now he fixes everybody's cars.

    Marshall made gumbo and gave me a party with all my friends from when he was the sweetheart of the club. We had a great time, except I drank too much. I am not and have never been and never will be a hard drinker. Two glasses of wine is really all I can drink. I had lost weight and bought myself some Gloria Vanderbilt jeans. They fit like a glove, and I had on my heels with a cute hat. The skycap asked me where I was going and if he could go too. I laughed and was flattered. I met Albert in Singapore. I was disappointed that he didn't acknowledge my weight loss or how I looked. Even one of the sales clerks asked where I got those jeans. I later found out why. He was only concerned with buying the things for which people had given him money. We were staying in the Hyatt Regency in Singapore in a private suite. That hotel belonged to a person whom Albert had helped get a government contract. The Chinese were never considered for government contracts, and when Albert got himself one, he was forever indebted. The day after I arrived, we had stationery printed in gold and put it in our room. It had our names on it. We also had a private waiter at the end of the hall for any of our needs. Albert didn't know that our accommodation had been paid for, and when we checked out, he said I wonder if we have enough money. They informed us that our bill had been paid and thanked us for staying at the Hyatt. We were ecstatic.

    The children were so glad to see me, and in spite of having Geneá's hair braided, it was a mess. Albert never told their teachers that I was not in Indonesia, and their grades reflected it. When I returned, we stayed in Embassy housing. Somehow, before I returned, Suhardi found out we were back, and he was there working. Kartini did not return, and we had to get another baba cuci and jaga. The house was a complex of houses that made almost a circle from one street to another. Behind our house was the clubhouse and swimming pool. We got in trouble with the neighbors right away. We weren't supposed to burn our trash; unlike other places in Jakarta where we lived, they came and collected our trash. They informed us of this, and we informed our servants not to burn, but for some reason, they did anyway. They had never lived in this type of environment, so I understood, but I did tell them that they could not, under any circumstances, burn the trash. I even had Henny come and repeat it in Bahasa Indonesia. I guess the next-door neighbors who told us not to burn thought we were not respecting the rules, so they reported us and caused a rift right away. This was a large house with a living room, dining room, and family room all in one big, long, and wide room. The embassy gave each person money to furnish their house. We had four bedrooms and two bathrooms. Albert had met the Blues, and we all became fast buddies, although they were much younger than we were. Josephine was pregnant when I met her, and they had a son named Dwight. He was so cute, and we all loved him. We fell into a routine of them coming over and playing cards. I had been home for about three weeks when Josephine and her husband, whom we called Blue by his last name, came over. We were sitting around talking about various things. All of a sudden, my foot began to cramp and hurt really badly. They said for me to go and put it up and have Suhardi put ice on it, and to call them later to tell them how I was doing. I did that, and in about an hour, I picked up the phone to call them and heard Albert on the phone. I put it down and waited. I noticed he did not come in to check on me or see how I was doing. I waited and picked up the phone again, and he was still on it. So, I decided to listen, and I heard, "I don't want her, I want you." That was all I heard, and I came out of the room, and he saw the jig was up. All of the ignoring came to light. He had been having an affair with Sandra. She was married to the third most powerful man in the country. She was his niece. Needless to say, I wanted to come home and start divorce papers. I talked to his boss.

"What does the contract state for me to leave before the contract is up?"

"Has Albert been drinking?" he asked.

"Yes," I answered.

"Will you wait until I get back to you?" he probed.

I had Suhardi put all of Albert's clothes into the spare room. Suhardi was so confused that he hesitated to do it until Albert told him to do so. I told Josephine and Blue, and they were all sad about it. I didn't want to live with him anymore or subject our children to this behavior. He told our son he had nothing to do with it. I told him he had every right to be angry, and if it was affecting him, he had every right to have something to do with it. My eyes were swollen shut from crying—the idea of bringing her over here to cheat on me. I was not only hurt but embarrassed, and I really didn't know if I wanted to stay with him or not. We were supposed to be godparents to Dwight that Sunday, and even with ice and cold towels, I had to wear sunglasses.

I didn't hear from Albert's boss. I decided to call this Sandra and confront her.

"Sandra, you don't know who you're fooling with. I'm a Black woman, and I don't play games like other women. I think I'll call your husband, and," she began to stutter, swearing she didn't know what I was talking about. "Under no circumstances are you to get in touch with my husband, and do not send your little girls here to find out from him what was going on. "I have people where Albert works that will report to me if you make contact."

She tried everything to get him to talk to her. She had one of the girls in the office call regarding some business. I told her to tell her boss she had no business with her and not to call again. All of the ignoring me came to light.

Unfortunately, I was not the only wife who was having that problem, and some of them actually got divorced from their husbands. It seems that when someone strokes your ego and is willing to do anything you want for a small amount of money, that becomes the perfect environment to cheat and think you're on top of the world. The oil companies, in particular, had a big problem. They began to really interview candidates and see where they were in terms of family and values. I told Albert the only way we would be together is if he went with me to a therapist. He balked. "I don't want to discuss my business with anyone."

"Okay. When we go back home this time, I will not be coming back, and you can do as you please," I warned.

"I'll talk with our pastor at the church," he capitulated. I agreed.

When we got home, we talked to the pastor, and he had nothing to say. The pastor said, obviously, there was something he was displeased with. He agreed that everything I told the pastor was true, and the only problem he had was that the car was sometimes late picking him up. Can you imagine someone as smart as Albert was, and that was all he could come up with? Most men really don't want another person knowing their business.

    We talked and I told him I was not satisfied with the sessions, and he would have to do better with convincing me that he was sorry and not cheat again. I told him I would not run after him as his first wife had. All I wanted from him was child support. I also told him I would never keep his children from him. Well, he apologized in a way that did not admit guilt, but we both agreed that if it ever happened again, I would walk, and there would be no more talk.

    When we returned, I found out that a lot of Americans were teaching English and bringing in extra money. I somehow found a lady named Ms. Budiono. She was Chinese, married to an Indonesian. They had two children, a boy and a girl. They were also very rich and stayed in the Ministry complex. He was awarded the contract to build a new airport, and he also owned other businesses. She soon asked if I could instruct her son, and I did. He was trying to get into a university in the States. He had a beautiful two-seater Mercedes that required special permission to bring into the country. We would ride around in it, and people would almost run into walls staring at us, and we would laugh. He was spending a lot of money to attend a university in the States, but people were taking his money, and he was going nowhere. I told Albert about him and his situation. By being in the UN, Albert could give the test he needed to apply for schools. He always missed them by 1 or 2 points according to the people that were helping him get into school. Albert gave him the test, and he passed. Albert then had him apply to the University of Hawaii, and he was accepted. I need to tell you how grateful they were. Ms. Budiono bought me a real Gucci bag. It was the first time I knew that a bag was sold in a bag. My granddaughter is now sporting it, and I can't get it from her. She says everybody admires that bag. I bet. I also taught Marie Masuda from Japan. She was in an arranged marriage and was very interesting to talk to. She was very tiny, and her husband treated her as I guess most Japanese men treat their women. It is a cultural and accepted custom. I later got a job at the American Indonesian Lembaga School. I guess I was becoming known. Most of the students that I taught knew grammar, but they didn't know our culture, and so in speaking the language, it was lost in translation because they had no concept of our culture. I would spend 20 minutes in each class, and I would go to different classes every week. The teachers would always tell me, "They have been expecting you." Everybody wanted to learn the language of money (English). We met a young man named Dawi, and he wanted to learn but didn't have any money. He worked for the International School, but he wasn't from Jakarta and was having trouble finding a place to stay and learning English. I offered him to stay with us, and he was thrilled. It was intimated to Albert that they didn't think it was a good idea to let an Indonesian live in our home. I asked if they couldn't or was this a suggestion. Our next-door neighbors reported everything that went on in our house. I worked at the Embassy teaching typing and English. They would send a car for all of us, and I was asked how I got a job there. I told them they needed to ask my husband or his boss. I felt really intimidated by them because they were all snobs and didn't like contractors. Contractors made twice what they made, so they did everything they could to not be friendly. I really didn't care because we had so many friends and people coming in and out. We had a friend from Vietnam, who was married to an American working in oil. She was too funny, and the women around the pool would talk about her viciously. She would tickle us by saying, "I tell him once, I tell him two times, he's just a mother-------." The funny part was that she was trying to curse and couldn't pronounce the words. We would laugh at Lee, not at her, but with her. We were the rebels around the American club. We had an anniversary party, and the police had to block off the street. There were so many people. We had a lady from Hawaii who did the hula. We had dancers and singers from Sumatra. Before the party, my house looked like a florist's. We really had a good anniversary this time. Albert did the funky chicken, and they all laughed. We fed and served everybody, including the police. I was completely exhausted when it was over. One of the things that I miss is waking up from a bash like that, and it looked as if it never happened, except for the flowers. Harry came that Christmas, but Angela didn't; I can't remember why. Again, Suhardi loved Harry and talked about him coming until he got there.

    We would go to the beach, and this one beach was on the Indian Ocean. They had stories that even intellectuals believe. They said there was a Sea Queen and she loved the color green, so we were not to wear the color green. The hotel there had a room that was not used because the Sea Queen lived in it. Now you know that this is folklore, but for some reason, we tend to think it may be true. Geneá was the only one of us that had some green flip flops. We were all talking and getting our food when suddenly I didn't see Geneá. Well, you know what I was thinking. We ran up to the hotel, where they had showers to get the sand off, and we looked and asked people if they had seen her. I was frantic. We started back to the group, and I spotted her. She was having fun and not thinking about us. How she got back from the bathhouse without us seeing her was a mystery. Anyway, I told her she was never to do that again. We also would go to another beach and stay in the cabin that one of our friends had. One time we went, and there was a mix-up, and someone else was using the house. They apologized, and we also. It was fate that we did not stay. When we returned home, our Jaga had unplugged and wrapped up our stereo unit. When he saw us returning, he ran, but we didn't know what was going on until we went inside. Of course, Suhardi didn't see. They would never tell on each other. There are always exceptions because the Jaga where Suhardi worked told his boss that Suhardi had stolen his money, which is why he didn't have his ID. He had to report every week, and they would interrogate him. That's why he was so grateful to Albert. Suhardi was an exceptional person and servant. He was our cook and all-around servant. He always smiled and never complained. He would take orders from the children and Mr. Brown, but not from me. This was the only thing we would clash. He had a running account with the vendors on the street for the children. They knew they were not supposed to be eating off the streets. The street vendors would wash their dishes in the puddle of water in the streets. Indonesia did not have sewers, and when it rains, you would have to wait until the rats and other vermin go back underground. We had to boil our water and apply Lugol's solution to our vegetables. Not only did I not want them to eat off the street vendors, but I also did not want a running bill with them.

  During Ramadan, all debts must be paid, and you must provide your servants with new clothes and money. Suhardi came and said we owed the street vendor. I asked him how much it was and gave him the money to pay them, and when he returned, he did not give me the correct change. He insisted that he did. It ended up with me firing him. Albert was so upset because he was losing a servant who waited on him hand and foot. So, Albert brought him back in, and we had a truce, and we were fine. Suhardi was the most gentle person that I have ever known, and if I could have brought him back with me, I would have. His wife was crazy, and Suhardi knew it. He was surprised when she came to see him. She lived far out, and for her to come into the city was a big thing. Suhardi was always embarrassed around her. She didn't think we should be treated in the manner that we should. I only spoke to her once and she just glared at me. He had beautiful children. Suhardi would always shower and put on clean clothes to serve us dinner. One day, our interpreter friend came to see us, and she began to talk to Suhardi, and he looked as if she were speaking Greek. Until she began to speak on his level, and he was so dumbfounded to hear a white woman speak his language so well. I often think about him and know that he is probably dead. We went to Bali. The capital city is Denpasar, and nearby is Sanur, a coastal resort area that was more affordable. We stayed in the Sanur area, and the little cottages were right on the beach. They had thatch roofs and a gazebo where you could sit, and at night, the water was close; you could feel it on your feet. The children were mesmerized by the sight. The Sanur side is less metropolitan than the Denpasar side. We took a becak (a three-wheeled pedicab) to a famous wood carver, and when we were sitting in this little crowded car, one of the Indonesians thought I was an easy catch to steal from. He insisted that I let him read my palm, and I noticed that I felt something in my side like someone was going into my purse. When we were about to get off, I checked to see that all of our money was gone. I stood and told him to give me my money, which he had stolen. I guess I performed so badly that he dropped it and then tried to rush us out of the car. I called him a few names, and he banged on the top for the driver to quickly move. I was going to report him.

    Bali is heaven on earth. It is so lush, and they have beautiful temples. They have some of the most credited people in woodworking that you have ever seen. Every evening, the people would dress in beautiful costumes and carry food on their heads to offer to the gods. It was a beautiful procession. The old women didn't wear tops and sat just as normal with their breasts exposed. We saw a funeral procession, and that was truly a treat. We went to the famous Chicak dance. If you sit on the beach, some masseuses come and massage you. The children truly enjoyed Bali. In our travels, we went to the Philippines, Bangkok, Singapore, but Bali was the most impressive.

    Later, Albert's sister came and wanted to take Albert to Bali. He didn't want to go, so I was second best. She took me. We also had a wonderful time. We went to Jogjakarta on the train because Inka had a house there. It is also a place where you can order brass gongs. They were beautiful. Albert had the opportunity to travel more than we did due to his work. He went to Sumatra and Irian Jaya. Both places are unique. In Sumatra, there are the Batak people, who are a patrilineal society and are famous for their beautiful singing voices. In West Sumatra, the Minangkabau are a matrilineal society, one of the largest in the world. They remind me of Africans because when they sing, the harmony is out of this world. Irian Jaya (now called Papua and West Papua) is the western half of the island of New Guinea.

The eastern half is Papua New Guinea, an independent nation. They have a fascinating culture. They have wars every day, but if someone gets hurt, the war is stopped. The women wear grass skirts and necklaces. I have a necklace from a man named Moses. He was Irian, and he looked exactly like us. He came to Jakarta and we met him. He was very good-looking and didn't look like the average Irianese. He brought me back the necklace that belonged to his mother. The Indonesians treat them similarly to the way Black people are treated in the U.S. The men wore a koteka, which is a gourd on their private parts. The longer the koteka, the richer they were. They would grease themselves with pig fat to keep warm from the cold. They lived high up in the trees. Some of them, I'm told, are still cannibals. The missionaries came and wiped out a lot of them because they had them put on clothes, but never told them they needed to be taken off and washed. Many of them got diseases from the clothing and died. Part of the transmigration project Albert was working on included trying to relocate people from Java to inhabit some of the other islands.

As part of Indonesia's transmigration program, people from Java were resettled in areas such as Sumatra, Kalimantan, Sulawesi, and Irian Jaya. The government gave the new settlers houses, food, and land, which angered many Papuans who didn't receive the same benefits. This led to resentment and sometimes violent clashes, where some were killed. We were invited to the celebration for Papua New Guinea by the Nigerian Embassy. Victoria Fakokie invited us and sent us the most beautiful invitation. I went and wore my African outfit from Liberia, and all the African women were sitting together, just looking at me. Victoria was the only one who was hospitable. I started talking to one man, and I told him he looked like someone I knew in the States. He became indignant and said to me I'm Papuan. He left me standing there. I guess I insulted him, though I didn't mean to.

My Journey Through Life, Love, and Tragedy

    Our experiences in Indonesia are so vast that I can't remember them all. It was a wonderful five and a half years. I wanted to come home, and I didn't want to come home. Geneá adamantly did not want to come home. She loved and loves Indonesia still to this day.

    I think Albert got wind of Kevin being gay. His little friend's mother said that Ian couldn't come over anymore because he had to study. I found out from Geneá that a bunch of boys hemmed him in the office at the American Club. Geneá would fight, but she would never tell if he told her not to. I also found out he was sneaking next door to the enemy's house. Word and gossip began to circulate that he was gay. I truly had my head in the clouds because none of this became clear until he came out. Some of my friends say that I was in denial.

Hot Stuff

    I had lost down to a size eight and had a whole wardrobe made to bring home. I would dance every morning. It would tickle Suhardi, and I could see them sneaking and smiling at me. I was shopping and I would eat this tofu with this little chili pepper they called a cabe. It was so hot that if it touched your skin, it would burn. Not thinking and popping these things in my mouth, I got an ulcer. It had burned a hole in my stomach. I did the wrong thing and took an aspirin, and I really thought I was going to die. They had to get me on a flight to Singapore, and I checked into Glen Eagles Hospital. They ran all kinds of tests on me and even gave me a CT scan, and this was before the United States had a CT scan. When I brought the pictures to Stanford Hospital, they asked where I got them. They gave me a different medicine that began to ease the pain. Between the tests, they would let me go with Charlie around Singapore. He would take me to the noodle house and buy me gold earrings. We went and saw Tootsie. One time, while I was out, my sister called, and I was not there, and she said, "What kind of hospital lets you go to movies and things, and you are still a patient?" My brother Lester from Cincinnati called me, and I was quite surprised. When it was time for me to go, they presented me with the bill, and I called Albert. He told me he would get it as soon as possible. We had insurance, but our insurance paid after the bill had been submitted. He talked with Mr. Anwar, and he said how much it was. He not only paid it but sent his person to pay and a chauffeured limousine to pick me up. I went and got my medicine, and I asked if he would take me to McDonald's. That was a treat for us because, at that time, we didn't have anything but Kentucky Fried Chicken, and it came the year we were leaving. I couldn't get Albert on the phone to tell him exactly when I was coming home, so I had to take a taxi in the hope that he would be home, as I was flat broke. Thank God he was home, and they all came running to see me. The kids loved the McDonald's even though it was cold. Geneá told me later that she and Kevin thought that Albert had killed me because they didn't know where I was going. I honestly thought they knew and that I told them, but in confusion, sometimes you miss things. I apologized.

    We began to pack, and Suhardi knew this time we were not coming back. He cried so hard that my blouse was wet with tears when we left. He knew it was for good this time. We asked Ms. Budiono if she would send one of her cars for us, and she was glad to do it. She sent two Mercedes—one for us and one for our luggage.

    I truly loved living in Indonesia. I enjoyed the people and country on many levels. In some way, they reminded me of my earlier years in Memphis. They are the most hospitable people I have ever known. It didn't seem real that we were not coming back.

    We left, and everybody was crying. It takes two days to get here. We stopped in Hawaii, and Geneá, not knowing we were in the United States, screamed, "Can I drink the water?" When we arrived, the renters were still in our house. Harry had given them notice, but they really didn't want to move. We stayed with Melissa and Dan until I told them I had to have an operation, which I did, and I would need to get settled. We moved back into our house and began to get settled.

When we first arrived in Indonesia, Albert went to work right away. He never once acted like the boss but like one of the workers. He would work every Saturday and listen to their complaints. One was that the computers had the devil in them because they only spoke English. He went to Myron, the head of IBM, and had him change the language of the computer to Bahasa Indonesian language. Albert was so well-liked and respected that he was able to get an Indonesian contract from a Chinese Indonesian. The government didn't give contracts to the Chinese because they didn't like them for several reasons, but mostly because they were the tax collectors under the Dutch rule. The contract became well-known among the Chinese community, and Albert's status was even higher than before Mr. Anwar, who was awarded the contract. Mr. Anwar was the head of Texas Instruments. His wife's family owned the Hyatt Regency in Singapore.

We were introduced to a man in Singapore named Mr. Ho, who owned a glass company and had placed a bid, winning a contract to build a hotel and shopping center in Singapore. That was a very big deal because Singapore is a city-state and it is very short on land space. Mr. Ho ran out of money and couldn't go any further, so after hearing about Albert, he came to him to get him funding and save the project.

    Albert started working on it before we came home, and after we got home, he put himself into it 100 %. He started a company and brought together his sister, a CPA; his brother, a lawyer; Harry, our son; Al Fisch, a Protestant Jew; Charlie Tan, as another board member; and, of course, me. We worked day and night. Albert ran out of gas on the way home one night. We were so broke we had to use gas from the lawnmower, and we didn't have AAA Road Service. He was using every resource he had, and of course, he began to come under attack when things weren't working out. My friends began to whisper that this wouldn't come to fruition because it was too big. Al Fisch's godson said it wouldn't work because we had dolls in the house that had been used in satanic rituals. Others were saying that they would give us the money, but we had to make Albert's sister CEO. Others were saying he needed the white guys to represent him. Poor Mr. Ho was being courted by large investors, but he wouldn't budge. We suggested that he seek another source, but he chose to stay with us. Albert was finally able to get a legitimate backer in San Francisco. The money was put into a bank in Singapore, and the president asked Charlie Tan how much more money would be coming through the bank. He was a friend of Mr. Anwar. Instead of his saying you will have to talk to the president, he said, "Oh, millions." The banker became afraid that he wouldn't be able to handle that much money at one time. Consequently, he performed a deposit reversal, withdrawing the money from the bank. I left work a millionaire and got home a pauper.

    Unfortunately, Mr. Ho went to prison because at that time, Singapore still had debtor's prisons. He died not long after getting out. While Mr. Ho told us that he didn't hold us responsible, that was and is a thorn in our side. It also raised the question of whether God has favorites, as our friends were successful in their business ventures, and we were right back where we started. It makes you wonder.

Part 14

Across the Generations

Chapter 30: Understanding Our Differences

I never thought I would live this long. Yet here I am, holding on to breath and memory, trying to leave you the last of my story before those, too, slip away. One day, I may not even know my own name.

I once gave my children a poem and a list of thank-yous. Those gifts still stand. But life has carried me into a place so different from what came before that I must add this chapter, if only to set the record straight.

In these later years, I have searched for answers—why we seem so disconnected, why we struggle to meet one another across the gaps of time. My search led me back to the generations, each with its own voice, its own burdens, its own way of being.

On August 20, 1619, the first recorded enslaved Africans were brought to English North America, landing at Point Comfort, Virginia—a beginning that would shape my ancestors, my family, and ultimately me. I share this history not only so you can trace the generations that came before me, but also so you can see why we bore the names we did, and how those names tell stories of endurance. If you take the time to study this history alongside my book, you'll begin to see me—and my people—with greater clarity.

Does God Have Favorites?

The listing of these generations starts with the Arthurian Generation (1433-1459) and goes all the way to 2051

Humanist Generation (1460 -1482).
Reformation Generation (1483 – 1511).
Reprisal Generation (1512 – 1540).
Elizabethan Generation (1541 – 1565).
Parliamentary Generation (1566 – 1587).
Puritan Generation (1588 – 1617).
Cavalier Generation (1618 – 1647).
Glorious Generation (1648 -1673).
Enlightenment Generation (1674 – 1700).
Awakening Generation (1701 – 1723).
Liberty Generation (1724 – 1741).
Republican Generation (1742 – 1765),
Compromise Generation (1767 – 1791),
Transcendental Generation (1792 – 1821).
Gilded Generation (1822 – 1842).
Progressive Generation (1843 – 1859).
Missionary Generation (1860 – 1882).
Lost Generation (1883 – 1900)

    My mother belonged to what historians call the Lost Generation. They came of age in the shadow of World War I, when so much of the world felt disoriented and adrift. She carried that heaviness with her, and I, as her child, felt it, too.
    I was born into what they call the Greatest Generation, though some also call it the Silent Generation (1925–1945). Silent because so many were expected to conform, to fall in line. When I read that, it startled me, because it explained why my life felt so different. I have never been one to conform—that restless spirit of mine is one reason I so often drove my mother to distraction.

The Greatest Generation (1901–1927)
1. Patriotic and Civic-Minded — Fought in WWII or contributed on the home front. Strong sense of duty.
2. Disciplined — Grew up in scarcity; learned frugality, order, and perseverance.
3. Community-Oriented — Believed in collective effort over individual recognition.
4. Loyal to Institutions — Trusted government, military, and established organizations.
5. Resilient — Overcame economic and wartime hardship with determination.
6. Hardworking — Valued long hours and steady work as a moral responsibility.
7. Traditional Family Roles — Emphasized stability, marriage, and clearly defined gender roles.
8. Respect for Authority — Deference to leadership in workplaces, families, and communities.
9. Conservative with Money — Lifelong savers due to Depression-era scarcity.

The Silent Generation (1928–1945)
1. Conformist — Grew up under social pressures to fit in, avoid rocking the boat.
2. Hardworking — Valued steady careers, many stayed with one employer for life.
3. Traditional — Maintained strong family structures and conventional morals.
4. Civic Duty-Oriented — Believed in contributing to society through stability and service.
5. Rule Followers — Respectful of authority, institutions, and hierarchy.
6. Financially Prudent — Conservative spenders, careful savers.
7. Politically Moderate — Often leaned toward compromise rather than extremes.
8. Disciplined — Preferred order, schedules, and avoiding conflict.
9. Sacrificial — Placed duty to family and community above individual desires.

Does God Have Favorites?

After us came the Baby Boomers (1946–1964), sometimes known as the Jones Generation. They earned that name from the saying "keeping up with the Joneses"—always striving, always competing. I knew competition, too, but mine was different. I never measured myself against neighbors or friends. In fact, I often thought it was the other way around—that others were trying to keep up with me.

Baby Boomers (1946–1964)
1. Idealistic — Inspired by the 1960s counterculture, civil rights, and social change.
2. Work-Centered — Defined identity through career achievements.
3. Competitive — A Large cohort created competition for jobs and opportunities.
4. Optimistic — Raised during economic expansion, expected progress.
5. Value Success and Status — Measured success in financial terms and upward mobility.
6. Team-Oriented — Used to collaboration in large organizations.
7. Revolutionary — Pushed cultural shifts in music, politics, and gender roles.
8. Goal-Driven — Sought financial security and home ownership.
9. Resistant to Retirement — Many remain active in work and community life longer than expected.

The next Generation is called Generation X (1965-1980). They are (disambiguation). I have to number them: The only ones I can question are those who adapt to new technology. If the technology is computers, then I am not. The other is Least Parental. I can't say that I am or was, because I certainly didn't have the same level of freedom to act and speak as my kids did. I don't know even today if I was. Number one, I am sometimes accused of not acting my age or dressing in my era, which I never will.

Generation X (1965–1980)
1. Thirteenish — An in-between identity, too old to be kids, too young to be adults.
2. Highly Independent — Many were latchkey kids, fostering self-reliance.
3. Value Work and Balance — Prioritize career stability with personal life.
4. Adapt to New Technology — Witnessed the shift from analog to digital.
5. Resilient — Shaped by recessions, layoffs, and changing social norms.
6. Open to Constructive Feedback — Value practical, honest input.
7. Like to Learn New Skills — Embrace lifelong learning to adapt.
8. Least Parental Generation — Fewer children, more pragmatic parenting.
9. Least Resistant to Change — Flexible and adaptable in cultural and technological shifts.

Millennial Generation called Generation Y. They are called Millennials because the oldest of this group was born at the turn of the century. Here are some of the qualities of the Gen Y. When it comes to this generation, their purpose-oriented, self-driven, and flexible nature is about all I can relate to.

Millennials (1981–1996)
1. Digital Natives — First generation to grow up with the internet.
2. Purpose-Driven — Seek meaningful work aligned with personal values.
3. Collaborative — Comfortable working in teams and networks.
4. Diverse and Inclusive — Value social justice, inclusivity, and multiculturalism. They are the most charitable.
5. Experience-Oriented — Value experiences over possessions.
6. Feedback-Seeking — Desire frequent coaching and input.
7. Entrepreneurial — Pursue side hustles or startups.
8. Debt-Burdened — High student loans and financial strain.
9. Work-Life Integration — Seek flexibility and remote work options.

These groups are getting further and further from the way I lived when I was their age. Most of what we can say about this group and me is the charity, and I also read that they spend about 85% of their time on mobile devices. Lately, I can say, me too.

Generation Z (1997–2012)
1. True Digital Natives — Entire childhood shaped by mobile tech and social media.
2. Pragmatic and Realistic — Cautious after Millennials' debt challenges.
3. Financially Minded — Saving-oriented compared to Millennials at the same age.
4. Diversity as Norm — Most racially, ethnically, and gender-diverse generation.
5. Independent Learners — Use online platforms for education.
6. Activist-Oriented — Passionate about climate, equity, and justice issues.
7. Mental Health Aware — Open about anxiety, depression, and well-being.
8. Entrepreneurial Spirit — Influencers, content creators, side hustlers.
9. Short Attention Spans — Prefer quick, visual, interactive content.

Generation Alpha (2013–2025)
1. Born Digital — First raised entirely with smartphones and tablets.
2. AI-Native — Grow up alongside artificial intelligence and smart devices.
3. Pandemic Shaped — Socialization and schooling influenced by COVID-19.
4. Global Perspective — Connected to worldwide issues from early age.
5. Highly Educated — Expected to be the most formally educated generation.
6. Environmentally Conscious — Raised in a climate-aware era.
7. Health & Safety Focused — Parents emphasize well-being and safety.
8. Visual & Interactive Learners — Prefer gamified and video-based learning.
9. Family-Centric but Independent — Involved parents yet self-directed tech use.

This research is far from being complete, so if you fall into any of these groups, do not be offended if some of the information may be wrong or if you don't agree. I did not do the research for accuracy as much as comparability.

I find that no matter when or where you were born, it is important that you know who you are and that you have values that are indicative of humans.

I never thought of age except the age of 30. Because I was so far behind my brothers and sisters, the most I heard from them was that life was over at 30. I remember calling my sister, and she asked what was wrong. I told her I was happy to have lived to be 30, but I felt like my life was over. She said, "You damn fool, I'm 50, so why are you complaining?" Again, no sympathy for what I was feeling, just that I think she wished she were 30 again, and here I come moaning about being 30. She did not understand my view at all. Again, living past 85 means that my youngest brother and I have outlived all of our siblings.

The Epilogue

    The one thing I always said I never wanted to be is dependent on anyone. I am so particular about everything, especially food. I am somewhat at that point in my life, and I'm dreading it. Because I never want to seem ungrateful, but there are some things I just can't eat unless they are a certain way. The other thing that reminds me of my age is my husband's illnesses. He was always as healthy as a horse, and all of a sudden, he started with bladder cancer, then COVID-19, then pneumonia, and he passed out at work and took a long time to revive. When he got over that, he fell and broke his hip and pelvis, plus he was diagnosed with leukemia. The worst thing is that after a long period of being unable to work, we are drowning in bills. Therefore, I urge anyone reading this book to set aside some money, no matter how small. Everyone kept saying he shouldn't have been working anyway. What I can't get everyone to understand is that earlier, when we first married, he said, "Cora, I'm going to work until I die." Albert worked until he could no longer do so. He was a wonderful provider and supporter of my goals. I hoped he'd be able to see this book in print before he passed on. We had a long talk about things. It warms my heart to remember that before his condition declined to the point where he no longer recognized me, he affirmed his support for me one last time, "Promise me that you will not let my condition change anything. Keep your plans to launch your book on your birthday."

    After 57 years together, on August 28, 2025, he passed away.

    As I struggled through the grief of the moment, a minister gave me this poem:

When you lose a parent, you lose the past. When you lose a friend or partner, you lose the present, and when you lose a child, you lose the future.

I thought that was so awesome because it's so true. Albert enjoyed his work. I couldn't get people to understand that when you enjoy something, it isn't a chore. He always loved computers; he had a degree in Computer Science and a Master's in Education. He loved sharing his knowledge with kids, especially the young ones who hadn't been exposed to a lot of life. I enjoyed living life with him.

I never thought about arthritis, falls, knee replacements, hip replacements, or any other illness that may befall you. I was too busy dancing to think of any of those things. I don't want you, the reader, to think I'm being morbid or that you shouldn't enjoy life to its fullest, but remember that in life there is a tomorrow, and you want it to be as carefree as possible. That's why I mentioned all the things I did.

The same daughter that I wrote about earlier is now, along with her brother Harry, my biggest help, and I am grateful to them. Although I try to get them to understand that I enjoy things, I have bought things that make me happy. All I ask of them, or any of you who are in a similar situation, is to think of the person you are helping, not merely what you think is best.

Life is one of the greatest gifts that God gave us, and it doesn't depend on anyone but yourself to make it beautiful. Sometimes life is like my title, you wonder if you are favored or just one of the crowd. Not any more or less. That's why I hope that everyone reading this book will gain some value from the experiences I've shared. I researched the generations because each of those generations played the greatest part in our differences. Each generation seemed to have the good and the not-so-good. Each generation seems to demonstrate that humans are humans, regardless of when they are born. Some are born with good hearts, some with cold hearts, and some with no heart at all. I hope that the reader will take this book as my story, not your story.

My Journey Through Life, Love, and Tragedy

    May it help and inspire you to share your story, for all of us have one. I'm hoping that our beautiful young girls and ladies know that they are the most beautiful creatures God made, whether you are white as snow or black as tar, you are beautiful. Think of yourselves as flowers. In Seattle, I went to a tulip festival and went up on a platform to see all the species and colors of the tulips. It was one of the most memorable and beautiful sights I have ever seen. They were in all colors and all of the splendor; not one color was better than the other, but a bouquet of loveliness. Think of yourself as that bouquet.

    Never ever put yourself in a position where you are being used merely as a commodity for the good or enjoyment of others. Although you may live in the so-called ghetto or even the streets, that does not define who you are, and never let anyone else define who you are. Think. Who are they? Just because they took the position that they are better than you? Consider what I am saying; they *took* the position. Don't you give it to them, because that is the only reason they think they have it. Always remember, since you were born, you have been recording. When you feel blue, always put on a happy tape. Choose your day. Choose your life.

In the end,
whether we are The Favorite or we are just Favored,
we are all God's children,

Bibliography

Cowley, Malcolm. *Exile's Return: A Literary Odyssey of the 1920s*. Viking Press, 1934.

Fitzgerald, F. Scott. *Echoes of the Jazz Age*. Scribner's, 1931.

Hurston, Zora Neale. *Their Eyes Were Watching God*. J. B. Lippincott, 1937.

Hughes, Langston. *The Big Sea: An Autobiography*. Alfred A. Knopf, 1940.

Brokaw, Tom. *The Greatest Generation*. Random House, 1998.

Howe, Neil, and William Strauss. *Generations: The History of America's Future, 1584 to 2069*. William Morrow, 1991.

Wilson, William Julius. *The Truly Disadvantaged: The Inner City, the Underclass, and Public Policy*. University of Chicago Press, 1987.

Jones, Landon Y. *Great Expectations: America and the Baby Boom Generation*. Coward, McCann & Geoghegan, 1980.

Hooks, Bell. *Where We Stand: Class Matters*. Routledge, 2000.

West, Cornel. *Race Matters*. Beacon Press, 1993.

Coupland, Douglas. *Generation X: Tales for an Accelerated Culture*. St. Martin's Press, 1991.

Howe, Neil, and William Strauss. *13th Gen: Abort, Retry, Ignore, Fail?*. Vintage Books, 1993.

Dyson, Michael Eric. *Between God and Gangsta Rap: Bearing Witness to Black Culture*. Oxford University Press, 1996.

Howe, Neil, and William Strauss. *Millennials Rising: The Next Great Generation*. Vintage Books, 2000.

Fry, Richard. "Millennials Overtake Baby Boomers as America's Largest Generation." *Pew Research Center*, 25 Apr. 2016.

Clayton, Oba T'Shaka. *The Return to the African Mother Principle of Male and Female Equality*. Afrikan World InfoSystems, 1995.

Dimock, Michael. "Defining Generations: Where Millennials End and Generation Z Begins." *Pew Research Center*, 17 Jan. 2019.

Seemiller, Corey, and Meghan Grace. *Generation Z Goes to College*. Jossey-Bass, 2016.

Twenge, Jean M. *iGen*. Atria Books, 2017.

Gates, Henry Louis Jr. *Stony the Road: Reconstruction, White Supremacy, and the Rise of Jim Crow*. Penguin Press, 2019.

McCrindle, Mark. *The ABC of XYZ: Understanding the Global Generations*. UNSW Press, 2014.

Pew Research Center. "The Whys and Hows of Generations Research." *Pew Research Center*, 3 Sept. 2015.

About the Author

Cora Demetra Shannon-Brown was born a formidable 13-pound baby in Memphis's Hyde Park neighborhood in 1939, the youngest of nine children and the product of a tight-knit, faith-filled Black community that taught her how to endure and to dream.

Music became her passport out of poverty. After migrating to California as a teenager, she broke barriers at Berkeley High—earning the lead in the school's production of Babes in Toyland despite protests over a Black heroine and holding soloist spots in its elite choral ensembles.

Marriage and motherhood soon expanded Cora's stage to the wider world. She kept house and hope alive through nightly rocket attacks during the 1969 Tết Offensive in Saigon, Vietnam, and later navigated the rhythms of expat life in Jakarta and across Indonesia while raising three children.

Now settled back in Northern California, Cora sings and is the president of the Sojourner Truth Presbyterian Senior Choir. She enjoys being a mother to Harry, Paijoun, also known as Kevin, and Geneá; a grandmother to Anthony, Miles, Azaria, Chloe, and Téa; and a great-grandmother to Laila, Wynter, Gianna, and Luka.

Cora continues to sing with community choirs, mentors young women who "dream beyond the porch," and draws on over seven decades of grit, grace, and globe-spanning adventure. It's no surprise that after crafting the memoir you now hold in your hands, she plans to write even more.

www.ingramcontent.com/pod-product-compliance
Lightning Source LLC
Chambersburg PA
CBHW070053080526
44586CB00013B/1041